ANTHOLOGY OF TWENTIETH-CENTURY MUSIC

By the same author

Twentieth-Century Music:
A History of Musical Style in Modern Europe and America

The Norton Introduction to Music History

Anthology of TWENTIETH-CENTURY MUSIC

Edited with Analytical Comments by
ROBERT P. MORGAN

Yale University

W · W · NORTON & COMPANY

New York · London

The text of this book is composed in Bembo
with the display set in Bembo

Library of Congress Cataloging-in-Publication Data

Anthology of twentieth-century music / Robert P. Morgan, editor.
    p. of music — (The Norton introduction to music history)
    Includes index.
    1. Musical analysis—Music collections.   2. Music appreciation—
Music collections.   3. Music—20th century.   I. Morgan, Robert P.
II. Title: Anthology of 20th-century music.   III. Series.
MT6.5.A595   1991   91-24904

ISBN: 0-393-95284-3

W. W. Norton & Company, Inc.,
500 Fifth Avenue, New York, N.Y. 10110
W. W. Norton & Company Ltd.,
10 Coptic Street, London WC1A 1PU

Contents

Concordance with Morgan:
Twentieth-Century Music

Introductory Note

MEASURE NUMBER DESIGNATIONS

In references to musical events by measure number, occasional use is made of a "decimal" notation to indicate beats within the measure: in 3/8 meter, "m. 5.2" refers to the second eighth note of m. 5; in 4/4 meter, "m. 2.3" refers to the third quarter note of m. 2, and so on.

In scores with rehearsal numbers (nos. 9, 19, and 22), the rehearsal number itself is understood to indicate the bar line over which it stands. Thus, "rn 41" refers to the measure (or passage) beginning at rehearsal number 41; "rn 41 + 2" means the second measure after rehearsal number 41 (in effect, counting the measure beginning at the rehersal number as "1"); "rn 41 − 6" refers to the sixth bar before rehearsal number 41, etc.

PITCH DESIGNATIONS

In contexts requiring references to a specific octave register, C^4-B^4 designates the octave from middle C to B, C^5-B^5 the next higher octave, C^3-B^3 the octave below middle C, etc.

SET DESIGNATIONS

On the few occasions where references are made to set classes, these are indicated by pitch numbers (C = 0, C♯ = 1, D = 2, . . . , B = 11) within parentheses. Thus (0,1,2) indicates the set class consisting of C, C♯, and D, (0,3,4,6) indicates the set class containing C, D♯, E, and F♯, and so forth.

SCORE INSTRUCTIONS

All foreign language terms in the scores are translated in the Glossary beginning on page 444.

Preface

In preparing this anthology I had two principal considerations in mind: to provide a volume of music and analytical commentary supplementing my text *Twentieth-Century Music,* published in the Norton Introduction to Music History Series; and to provide a coherent, independent collection of pieces suitable for an undergraduate or graduate course in the analysis and literature of twentieth-century music. This dual function is reflected in the presence of the two tables preceding this Preface: one is a table of contents, in which the compositions are ordered as they appear in this book, according to composers' dates of birth; the other is a concordance with my historical survey, listing the works according to their place in the book's three-part chronological division. Both tables reflect essential and complementary facets of the selection process.

Among the many factors influencing that selection, the most important, aside from practical considerations of volume length and the availability of particular compositions, was the decision to use only complete works or movements (in the case of operas, complete scenes or sections). While this limited the number of pieces in the Anthology, it meant that all of them were complete entities rather than fragments. The limitation in number was partly countered, moreover, by the inclusion of a relatively large group of works for piano, voice and piano, and small chamber ensemble, and by the use of piano-vocal scores for operatic excerpts. Another influencing factor was my determination to emphasize major composers, and even include— in the case of a few figures who significantly influenced stylistic changes both before and after World War I—pieces from two different stages of their creative evolution.

The result, I believe, is a collection that is not only of unusually high quality but widely representative of Western concert music of this century. Included are twenty-nine works (or groups of works) by twenty-four different composers born in nine different countries; the works range chronologically from 1903 to 1983 and encompass every decade of the century but the last. All musical genres, which are indexed in the back of the book, are also represented.

The addition of analytical essays on each of the twenty-nine compositional entries distinguishes this Anthology from others in the Norton series.

They were written in the belief that since recent music poses special tech-nical problems for those lacking extensive analytical experience, many users of the volume would find such introductory commentary useful. Though the essays are necessarily brief and reflect my own particular musical and analytical interests, I have attempted to provide a general discussion of the overall form and character of the music in question. In some essays I have given a particular technical feature more detailed consideration, but I have tried to avoid highly specialized terminology where possible, and to explain its meaning and purpose when used. My hope is that the commentaries will encourage other, perhaps quite different, analytical approaches, and that readers will use them as points of departure for their own more detailed and particularized analyses.

Following the index of genres, you will find an index of analytical cate-gories, in which the musical forms and pitch and rhythmic attributes rep-resented in the compositions are listed. Although not exhaustive (readers are invited to add new categories and listings within categories), this index will be helpful to those wanting to compare similar musical features found in different styles and compositional contexts.

Most of the work on this volume was undertaken while I was writing the text for *Twentieth-Century Music,* which I completed while on the faculty of the Music Department at the University of Chicago. Once again, I thank my colleagues and students there, who played such an important part in the development of both volumes. Claire Brook and Suzanne La Plante of W.W. Norton aided in innumerable ways in seeing this Anthology to press. Among friends and colleagues at Yale, Jane Clendinning first brought Ligeti's *Wenn aus der Ferne* to my attention, Stephen Hinton made helpful suggestions concerning the translation of the Hölderlin text for that composition, and Allen Forte and Janet Schmalfeldt offered general support and stimulation. Particular thanks are again due to my friend David Hamilton, whose keen insight, editorial skills, and musical intelligence greatly enhanced the ana-lytical essays.

Robert P. Morgan
June 1991

1

CLAUDE DEBUSSY (1862–1918)
Estampes (1903), No. 2, *La Soirée dans Grenade*

ANALYTICAL COMMENTS

At first glance Debussy's *La Soirée dans Grenade* (Evening in Granada) seems little more than a "salon" piece evoking exotic dance music, a type much favored by popular composers around the turn of the century. Although the atmosphere and characteristic dotted rhythm of the Spanish habanera certainly contribute to the music's distinctive flavor, this is also a score of considerable subtlety. Its overall form is centered around three relatively extended, symmetrically distributed melodic units:

$$A \qquad B \qquad C \qquad B' \qquad A'$$
mm. 7–16 38–60 67–77 98–106 122–27

Equally important is the (usually varied) recurrence of several shorter units: *x* (mm. 17–20, 29–32, 92–97), *y* (mm. 23–28, 61–66, and, in diatonic form, 78–81), and *z* (mm. 33–36, 82–90). Over the course of the piece these shorter units tend to become longer, while the extended units become shorter.

Taken together, these seemingly individual and fragmentary components form a mosaic-like structure, quite unlike the forms associated with traditional tonality:

m.	1		7	17	23	29	33	38	61	67	78	82	92	98	109	122	130
	Introduction	*A*	*x*	*y*	*x*	*z*	*B*	*y*	*C*	*y'*	*z'*	*x*	*B'*	coda	(*A'*)		
key	C♯		C♯	C♯	C♯	F♯	F♯	A	C♯	F♯	C♯	C♯	C♯	A	—	C♯	F♯

One element unifying the diversity of melodic material is the almost constant habanera rhythm, introduced in the first measures, where it underpins a gradual expansion of pianistic range (a striking instance of Debussy's interest in composing out registral space). Even when it drops out (as in mm. 17–20 and 76–77), this accompanimental ostinato seems to persist beneath the surface. An elaborate system of melodic associations also helps bind the separate elements. The falling line of *A* is echoed both in *z* and *B*, while *z* also bears a strong rhythmic and melodic relationship to *C*. *C* in turn echoes

the rising line of *y*—a connection made explicit in m. 78, when *C* is immediately followed by *y* returning in diatonic form.

For all these multiple correspondences, each unit has its distinct identity,
attributable to differences in rhythm, texture, and pitch content. Yet even
pitch, viewed as a whole, is coherently structured. *A* is based on an "exotic"
symmetrical scale (Example 1a), while the top voice of *x* (accompanied by
parallel dominant-seventh chords) defines a modal scale (Example 1b) whose
four upper notes yield a similarly symmetrical whole-tone segment, identical to the corresponding segment of the exotic scale except that E♮ replaces
E♯. *Y* following *x,* is consistently whole-tone (Example 1c), except in its
final diatonic appearance. *B* and *C* are largely diatonic, *B* lightly and *C* more
heavily colored with chromaticism.

EXAMPLE 1

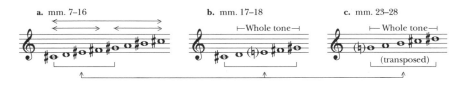

More general tonal correspondences support these pitch associations. Three
closely related key areas alternate in the piece: F♯, A, and C♯. Since the piece
ends on F♯, the C♯ areas might be said to represent dominants, and in fact
they all have an unmistakable dominant-like quality, underscored by
Debussy's tendency to use harmonic relationships laden with traditional tonal
suggestions. Yet the effect is quite different from that of a normal F♯ tonality, and although all three key areas are closely related, which one will emerge
as the final tonic is not clear until the end.

Since key areas are primarily established by pedal points rather than by
dominant-tonic progressions, one area gives way to another not by modulation in the traditional sense but by an almost instantaneous shift. For
example, the A-major focus of section *B* (m. 38) is achieved simply by
changing the F♯ pedal of the previous section to A in mm. 35–37; this move
is assisted by the placement of a chord on B major (rather than F♯ major) in
the right hand at mm. 35–36, weakening the finality of the cadential melodic
F♯. Instead of goal-directed progressions, Debussy uses relatively stable blocks
of motionless harmony; one key can give way to another without a strong
sense of pull in one particular direction. However, he does not totally shun
the evocation of tonal functions, and given the eventual emergence of F♯ as
tonic, it is surely significant that the work's only strong dominant-tonic
progressions occur at the beginnings of the three F♯ areas (mm. 28–29, 66–
67, 129–30).

The coda (mm. 109–36) is of special interest, consisting of almost dream-
like reminiscences of earlier bits and pieces, among which the return of *A*

(m. 122) is only the most extended. The recurrence of the first four measures of *C* (mm. 113–20) is bisected at m. 115 by the return of material unique to the coda (first heard in mm. 109–12), and *x* appears briefly in the left hand at mm. 128–29. Absent from the first part of the coda, the habanera rhythm returns sporadically in truncated form (m. 122), still weakly echoing as the music dies away.

The manner and speed with which the coda cuts back and forth among these fragments recalls film collage, a final intensification of the crosscutting techniques used throughout the work—which, indeed, resembles a picture made up of small, separate yet related parts, so connected that one seems to pass almost imperceptibly into the next. Recurring units are usually varied (for example, when *B* reappears at m. 98 it has a new accompaniment and new pedal bass, an E that links smoothly to the C-major opening of the coda), and all units seem able to lead to all others *(x* not only both precedes and follows *y,* for example, it also precedes and follows *z),* so that their formal context is constantly transformed.

2

RICHARD STRAUSS (1864–1949)
Salome (1905), Scene 1

ANALYTICAL COMMENTS

Strauss's *Salome* reflects the extent to which traditional tonal functions were undermined in certain works written during the first decade of the twentieth century. Although the first scene begins in C♯ minor—or at least on a C♯-minor chord—and returns to this chord near its end (m. 149), the chromatic voice-leading creates a shifting harmonic basis that calls into question the traditional notion of key as a hierarchical system of graded relationships.

Example 1, a harmonic reduction of the first major tonal progression, from C♯ minor in m. 1 to F major in m. 12, reveals how the chromatic linear motion stretches the triadic framework. Though it is still possible to find traces of an underlying root progression preserving traditional functions, from I to ♮III in C♯ minor (as noted below the example), extensive use of secondary dominants along with abundant linear elaborations within each harmonic unit create constant instability.

EXAMPLE 1

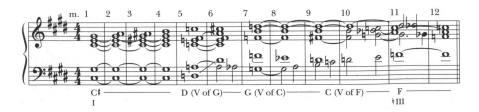

The scene nevertheless forms a distinct musico-dramatic unit, held together by essential, if often tenuous, harmonic, motivic, and formal correspondences. It begins without overture as the curtain rises. There are five main divisions, arranged like a rondo:

A	B	A'	C	A"
mm. 1–28	29–40	41–79	80–143	144–54

The first, third, and fifth sections, which share numerous musical correspondences and a common tempo, focus on Narraboth, captain of Herod's guard; he sings of the beauty of Salome (he can see her, but she does not appear onstage until Scene 2, the opening scene providing an extended preparation for her entrance), as his friend the page implores him to ignore her. In the first contrasting section *(B)*, which is faster, two soldiers comment on the noise from the neighboring banqueting hall. The second contrasting section, *(C)*, which is slower, introduces the voice of Jochanaan, imprisoned in a cistern and thus not yet visible, whose head Salome will eventually demand as reward for dancing for the king.

The opening segment features a motive that outlines the C♯-minor triad (mm. 1–2), preceded by a rising upbeat figure (which is developed separately in the final section). Associated with Salome, this motive appears prominently in each of the A sections (and only in these)—twice in A (mm. 1, 23), four times in A' (mm. 57, 62, 63, 64), and three times in A" (mm. 144, 147, 149); the motive makes one appearance in each section in the principal key of C♯ minor (mm. 1, 57, 149). (It can also be detected in the sixteenth-note figuration of mm. 46–51.) An important harmonic idea associated with the motive has a rising half step in the bass, usually with a descending half step in the voice or orchestra. It appears after each of the C♯-minor statements, as well as at other significant moments (e.g., the beginning of the first return of *A,* mm. 40–41).

All three A sections are characterized by rapid harmonic and rhythmic development. In the first two, Strauss directs the intense linear and chordal activity through ascending stepwise lines spanning extended segments of the score. Thus the top voice G♯^{5} of m. 1 proceeds upward chromatically to D^6 in m. 7, where the bass G^3 initiates a long climb, at first diatonic, that eventually passes through C♯^{7} in m. 28 to D^7 in m. 29 (omitted in the piano reduction), overlapping with the beginning of the B section.

The B and C sections are more stable harmonically. B appears entirely over a pedal bass D that, preceded by its dominant (mm. 27–28), provides a relatively clear D-minor focus, though with considerable dissonance and intense rhythmic activity throughout the section. C, despite rapidly shifting tonal areas, has clear triadic structures, functional harmonic progressions with diatonic voice-leading, and textures of almost chorale-like simplicity (associated with Jochanaan throughout the opera). Two related melodic figures connected with Jochanaan pervade the section, the first heard in mm.

82–84 (bass clef), the second mm. 86–91 (bass clef, combined with two statements of the previous figure in the treble). Though appearing in changing tonal and harmonic contexts, these figures do not undermine the relative simplicity of the section, a quality that sets it off sharply from the others. Also important is a rising minor-third figure introduced by Jochanaan in mm. 92–93 to the words "Wenn er kommt" (referring to the coming of Christ). This figure appears several times in the voice before being developed sequentially in the orchestral bass from m. 108 to the end, alternating with statements of the motive from m. 86.

Although most of the main melodic ideas have been mentioned, this discussion covers only the most salient aspects of the rich fund of brief motivic figures, whose complex interaction is, as much as the prevailing harmonic instability, responsible for the scene's high level of musical and dramatic tension. A common unifying factor among the disparate elements is the recurring interval of a sixth (usually major). It is first heard as part of the opening motive ($C\sharp^5$-E^4 in m. 1) and reappears, transposed, as the first two and last two notes of Narraboth's opening vocal phrase ($E\sharp^5$-$G\sharp^4$ in m. 3, inverted and respelled $A\flat^4$-F^5 in mm. 6–7). Most of the principal motivic ideas of the scene emphasize this interval: for example, the rising sixth figures first heard in mm. 5–7 (in the bass, C^3-A^3 at m. 5, $A\flat^3$-F^4 at mm. 6–7); the triplet figures in the upper register of the *B* section (A^5-F^6 at m. 29); and the opening, rising portion of the second main motive of the *C* section, outlining the sixth G^3-E^4 (m. 86). The new motive introduced to announce the beginning of Scene 2 (m. 155) also begins with a rising motion spanning a major sixth (E^4-$C\sharp^5$), forming a link with the previous scene.

In keeping with the Wagnerian leitmotif principle, all the important motivic units in Scene 1 recur at appropriate musical and dramatic moments throughout the opera. The initial "Salome" motive, for example, reappears almost immediately after Scene 2 begins (mm. 158–59), to mark the entrance of the anti-heroine, now initiating a more extended figure that descends triadically.

3

ALEXANDER SKRYABIN (1872–1915)
Piano Pieces

a. Prelude, Opus 35, No. 3 (1903)

b. Etude, Opus 56, No. 4 (1907)

c. Prelude, Opus 74, No. 3 (1914)

ANALYTICAL COMMENTS

These three pieces represent three stages in Skryabin's evolution away from traditional tonality in the early years of the twentieth century. The earliest, the Prelude, Op. 35, No. 3, is still triadic and tonal, although the tonic (C major) tends to be underplayed until the end of phrases. Thus, after appearing in first inversion as an eighth-note upbeat initiating the first phrase, C major does not reappear until the cadence in m. 11; the two tonic chords are connected by a series of four secondary dominant-to-tonic progressions linked by tritones:

EXAMPLE 1

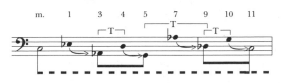

The emphasis on the tritone, although here essentially an extension of the traditional Neapolitan relationship (A♭ becoming the Neapolitan of G, D♭ the Neapolitan of C), has significance for Skryabin's later development, as it forms perhaps the most important component of the "mystic chord." Also notable is the liberal use of nonharmonic tones, often with extensively delayed resolutions (e.g., to the G♭ chord in mm. 13–14, resolving only after five beats).

Typically for Skryabin, the form of the Prelude, both its overall *A-B-A* design and its subdivisions, is quite schematic. In the *A* section, the first phrase consists of a six-measure subphrase plus its sequential transposition (slightly altered), and this entire phrase returns unchanged after a contrasting segment that is similarly made up of a six-measure subphrase and its sequential repetition (mm. 13–18, 19–24). The *B* section is equally repetitive: a twelve-measure phrase and its repetition (mm. 37–48, 49–60) are sequenced (mm. 61–72, 73–84), with a slight variation in mm. 70 and 82 to achieve a different harmonic goal (C instead of A♭). The *A* section returns literally at m. 85, except that the tonic upbeat is omitted (its function taken over by the final chord of the *B* section), and the final phrase is extended six measures to create a stronger close.

Despite the internal tritone progressions, the larger formal structure is unambiguously articulated by tonic-dominant root progressions. The phrases ending the outer sections, for example, cadence exclusively on the first and fifth scale degrees: G (m. 5), C (m. 11), C (m. 16), G (m. 22), G (m. 29), C (m. 35). Even the middle section, after first digressing to B♭ (mm. 48, 60), returns emphatically to the tonic C at its end (mm. 72, 84).

The Etude, Op. 56, No. 4, written four years later, stands suspended between the traditional tonal system and a new one. For extended stretches the tritone has become the principal interval of harmonic motion, linking altered dominant-type chords (similar to the "mystic" type) rather than fifth-related triads as before. The last dominant-type chord, on D♭ in m. 30, still receives a hint of traditional resolution when its repetition in the final measure is combined with outer-voice G♭'s, which supply a simultaneous tonic "resolution."

This implied fifth progression is anticipated in mm. 7–8.1 and 11–12.1, but in both places the resolution is also weakened by ongoing melodic motion in the top voice and by the resolving chord's noncadential position within the phrase. On the other hand, in mm. 17–20 (repeated 21–24) the sequence of root progressions by fifths (E♭-A♭-D♭-G♭, the last being a pure triad) lends the G♭ some degree of traditional tonal definition. But here too the G♭ chord's function as goal is obscured by melodic-rhythmic motion in the upper voice (especially in m. 24, where the chord moves back immediately to its dominant).

The formal arrangement is again straightforward, a symmetrical binary design: A (mm. 1–12)-A' (mm. 13–24), plus brief coda (mm. 25–31). The opening phrase initiates each of the three sections (mm. 1–4, 13–16, 25–27), followed each time by a different continuation: mm. 5–12, a four-measure unit and its sequential repetition a half step lower; mm. 17–24, a four-measure unit followed by a varied repeat (using the rhythm of mm. 5–8); and mm. 28–31, a two-measure interruption plus final cadence.

One of Skryabin's last works, the Prelude, Op. 74, No. 3, illustrates the composer at the height of his maturity. The underlying dominant-type sonority of the "mystic chord" is constantly enriched by chromatic additions, complicating the choice of a single version as basis for the entire piece. The minor-ninth version on F♯ (spelled upward in fourths: F♯-B♯-E-A♯-D♯-G) is the most likely candidate for the basic chord, and the piece does end with this chord.

A more efficient way to approach the Prelude, however, is to consider it in relation to the octatonic scale (alternating half steps and whole steps) on F♯, which contains all six pitches of the chord just mentioned:

EXAMPLE 2

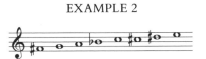

Every pitch in the work is drawn from this scale except the chromatic passing tones associated with the opening motivic figure in the right hand (G♯ in m. 1, D♮ in m. 3, G♯ in m. 5, etc.). A characteristic property of this scale is that when it is transposed by a minor third or tritone, it repeats the same sequence of intervals and same collection of pitches, a property Skryabin exploits in using only these two intervals to determine transpositions.

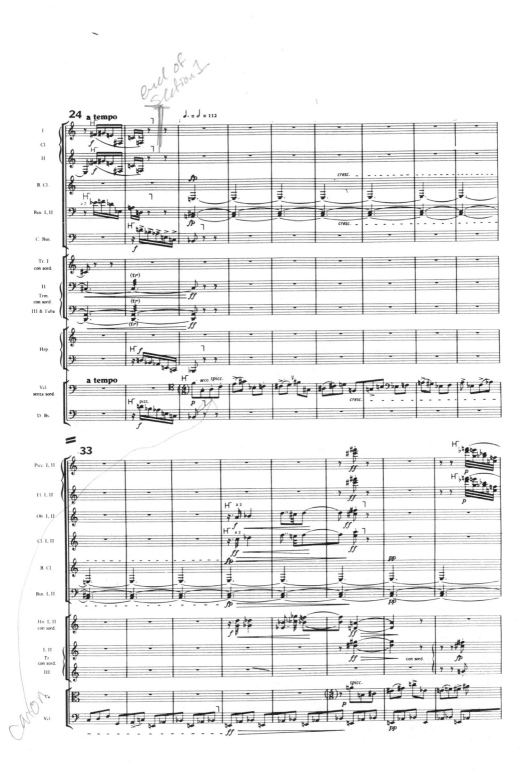

4

ARNOLD SCHOENBERG (1874–1951)
from Five Orchestral Pieces, Opus 16 (1909)

a. No. 1, *Vorgefühle* (Premonitions)

Thus the right hand of mm. 1–2 is sequenced up a tritone in mm. 3–4 (the added A in m. 4 is also scalar), while the left hand holds the tritone B♯-F♯ as a pedal. The right hand (plus the top voice of the left) is then sequenced downward through a series of minor thirds, its highest pitch moving A^5 (m. 4)-F♯^{5} (mm. 6–7)-D♯^{5} (m. 8)-C^5 (m. 9), while the left-hand tritone moves upward through minor thirds to D♯^{3}-A^3 (mm. 9–10) before dropping back to B♯^{2}-F♯^{3} in mm. 11–12.

The bass B♯ in mm. 11–12, formerly the upper member of the original left-hand tritone, becomes in m. 13 the lower member of that same tritone, part of an exact sequential restatement of the entire first section a tritone lower (mm. 13–24). Since the first section's bass moved a tritone from B♯ (m. 1) to F♯ (mm. 11–12), this transposition brings the motion back to its original point, completing the "circle" from B♯ to F♯ (the tritone divides the octave space equally). Thus the piece ends, after a brief pause and extension, on the same F♯ "root" with which it began. The phrases ending the two main sections (mm. 9–12 and 21–24, plus extension) fall entirely within the basic octatonic collection and present it in pure scalar form (mm. 12 and 24, repeated in part in m. 25), thus summarizing the piece's pitch content.

b. No. 5, *Das obligate Rezitativ*
(The Obligatory Recitative)

395

ANALYTICAL COMMENTS

These pieces illustrate two different phases of Schoenberg's atonal period. The first, composed somewhat earlier, is tightly constructed and relies heavily upon canonic devices. The second unfolds more freely and spontaneously, without systematic use of any generally applied structural principles.

Op. 16, No. 1, falls into two main sections of unequal length. The first (mm. 1–25) presents the basic materials, which the second (mm. 26–128) subjects to extensive development. The first important motivic idea, all of whose components—rhythmic, melodic, and harmonic—are explored in the piece, is stated at the outset:

EXAMPLE 1

The top line undergoes a number of relatively free melodic transformations, many involving inversion, in the first section: mm. 7–9 (double basses), 15–18 (cellos), 17–19 (flutes and English horn), and 22–23 (clarinets). The complete motive reappears transposed but essentially in its original form near the beginning of the second section (mm. 36–38, oboes, clarinets, and horns), then frequently thereafter in various extensions and transformations: mm. 48–53 (woodwinds), 63–68 (woodwinds and horns), 69–77 (piccolos, flutes, clarinets, and trumpet), 79–94 (horns), 95–105 (trumpets, later with horns). At mm. 106–9 the clarinet version from mm. 22–23 returns (trombones), transposed and sequentially extended, and the double bass version from mm. 7–9 reappears in that instrument at mm. 110–12, also transposed, producing a hint of reprise as the end approaches.

The thirty-second-note figure in the clarinets in mm. 4–6, derived from the sixteenth-note bassoon accompaniment of the initial motive, later appears (always in woodwinds) in mm. 20–22, 24–26 (in sixteenths), 40–42, 51–52 (inverted), 60–63, 105–6, and 120–28 (first in sixteenths, then in quarters). In the long stretch between appearances at mm. 60 and 105, its influence is recognizable in the thirty-second-note upbeat figures in mm. 68–76 and in the contour of the woodwind figuration in mm. 91–96. At three strategic points the motive leads to a repeating thirty-second-note figure: the end of the first phrase (m. 6, horn), the end of the first section (m. 22, trumpet— mm. 24–25 being transitional to the second section), and the beginning of the final subsection (m. 106, horn).

The second major section has three subsections: mm. 26–78, which develops to a massive climax; mm. 79–106, which takes off from this high point before gradually lowering the level of intensity; and mm. 106–28, which combines the functions of recapitulation and coda and, though largely static harmonically, expands texturally and rhythmically to the final cadence. All materials not directly related to the two principal motives of the opening section are derived from the steady eighth-note figure introduced by the cellos in m. 26 (itself intervallically related to the opening cello line in mm. 1–2). This figure reappears in canonic imitation a major third higher (with slight intervallic alterations) at m. 38 (violas, transferred to the upper cellos at m. 45), and a perfect fifth higher at m. 49 (second violins). Each entrance eventually congeals into a three-note ostinato figure.

The entrance at m. 49 is cut short for a climactic statement of the same figure at m. 57 (violins and upper violas), where only the first six notes are presented and then repeated before the line suddenly descends to a lower register to take up the three-note ostinato (both original and inverted forms), joining with the lower viola and cello ostinatos to produce a dense net of rhythmically staggered entrances. This is maintained until m. 73, when the line rises precipitously for the main climax.

In the second subsection the strings' canonic imitations are further intensified; only the first four notes of the original unit are used in ostinato-like fashion, and the interval of imitation is reduced first to a quarter note (m. 79), then to an eighth (m. 87, where there are four entrances within the measure). These imitations, all at the octave, produce a kind of harmonic "field," which breaks up after m. 91 when a series of sequential descents carries the strings into the lower register again. The three-note ostinato, taken up by harp and timpani in mm. 79–95, echoes briefly at m. 99, then continuously from m. 103 to the end (interrupted at mm. 121–24).

Other material derived from the canonic figure appears in mm. 60–62 (horns) and 79–95 (trumpets, xylophone, and trombones), with various rhythmic and melodic transformations, including augmentation and diminution. The melodic fragment heard in the first trumpets, flutes, and piccolos in mm. 54–56 is also derived from the figure (compare the cellos, mm. 30.2–31.1). The more extended line heard in the trombones (mm. 96.2–100.1) and strings (mm. 100.2–103.1), and also transposed and in diminution in the oboes, English horn, and clarinets (mm. 98–99 and 102–3), while not taken directly from the canonic figure (its more immediate forerunner is the horn figure from mm. 15–16 of the introduction), is related through a free retrograde process to the first part of the descent that marks the canon's dissolution in the upper strings in mm. 60–61: B♭-E-B-F becomes F-B-E♭-B♭.

Finally, the chord that closes the opening motive (see Example 1) provides a sort of harmonic center (though certainly not a tonic) for the piece. It is restated at the original pitch level, minus G♯, in the trombones at m. 23, picked up by the bass clarinet and bassoons at m. 26, and then sustained as a pedal (transferred back to the trombones at m. 113) through the remainder of the piece.

The fifth and last of the Op. 16 pieces is one of three compositions (the others are the Piano Piece, Op. 11, No. 3, and the monodrama *Erwartung*) written during a two-month period at the end of the summer of 1909, when Schoenberg, composing with unparalleled speed, reached the most extreme stage in his development away from traditional tonal, formal, and thematic conceptions. The music seems to have been conceived as a single gesture, a discursive "recitation" (Schoenberg entitled it *The Obligatory Recitative*) that, once underway, allows itself to spin out freely in ever-changing configurations.

Essential to the character of the piece is the complete absence of motives, in the normal sense of clearly defined rhythmic and melodic units that recur over extended stretches. Yet, despite the evolving, non-repeating quality, the score is full of veiled correspondences, the shadowy remnants of traditional motivic procedures. Occasionally these are immediately apparent, as in the recurring "accompanimental" figures in the flute (doubled by violin pizzicato) and clarinet, mm. 371–74. More commonly, they are hidden beneath the surface, where, too vague to be heard as explicit recurrences, they evoke only dimly perceived associations.

For example, the two subunits of the opening formal segment, mm. 331–37 and 337–47, begin similarly, the viola's opening E^5–$D\sharp^5$ figure answered by the cello's B^4–$B\flat^4$ in mm. 337–38 (with the closing downward glissando transferred to the lower cello). They also continue similarly (the clarinets in mm. 332–35 answered by the clarinets in mm. 339–44) and end similarly (the first violin's figure in mm. 336–37, elaborating a descending chromatic line doubled in the second violin, answered by the bass clarinet, bassoon, and cello figures in mm. 345–47, also elaborating a chromatic descent). All the figures but the last are marked with Schoenberg's H sign, indicating principal voice, while the last is exactly coordinated in duration with the H part in the first horn.

Similar "free associations" are found throughout the piece, contributing some degree of coherence despite the ongoing rush of events ensuing from Schoenberg's radical application of the idea of developing variation and musical prose. In addition, the larger flow is articulated into a formally convincing shape similar to the kind of climax-oriented designs found in Wagner and other late nineteenth-century composers. (In this respect, this movement resembles the first one.) Table 1 indicates the main divisions. Since the final segment of Section III functions as a kind of coda, the layout is almost symmetrical: three sections, each approximately forty measures in

TABLE 1

Section I	Section II	Section III
1. mm. 331–347.2	1. mm. 371–386	1. mm. 414–424.1
2. mm. 347.3–358	2. mm. 386–399	2. mm. 424.2–438
3. mm. 359–370	3. mm. 400–413	3. mm. 439–454
		4. mm. 455–466

length, each divided into three subsections. Moreover, the principal climaxes all appear at or near the end of the respective second subsections. Symmetry is weakened, however, by a cumulative development that spans the piece: each main section evolves more expansively than the preceding one. The first reaches its high point at m. 356, then quickly recedes; the second, after reaching an initial climax at m. 379, builds again to a higher point at m. 393, from which it retreats more gradually (though with an immediate, very dramatic drop in dynamics); and the third climaxes at m. 438, this time sustaining the level of tension through the entire first part of the third subsection (mm. 439–46). Each point of culmination is more intense than the previous one, with a higher dynamic level, greater density of texture, and more expanded registration (the top note, always played by the first violin, becomes progressively higher, for example).

These developmental processes are balanced by increasing finality at the close of the main sections. All three end with lengthening durational values, effecting a sort of written-out ritard, and with sustained chordal elements (notably absent elsewhere). The latter become more prominent with each closing section until they predominate during the final coda section, where the musical motion—relatively slow throughout the section—ultimately freezes into a sustained chord (mm. 463–66). (This last chord is still developed timbrally, an excellent example of Schoenberg's notion of *Klangfarben-melodie*.)

The wavelike motions of the three main sections, each beginning at a relatively low level of tension (soft dynamics, moderate registration, etc.), developing in complexity, and receding again to a point of relative rest, and each surpassing its predecessor in force and energy, produce a clearly audible overall shape. Yet this shape does not undermine the general quality of continuous evolution, certainly the work's single most characteristic attribute. The predominantly polyphonic conception generates linear strands with distinctly differentiated shapes, usually overlapping and interpenetrating one another, and the chamberlike scoring provides an almost unbroken web of fluctuating and intersecting textural patterns. Thus the segments indicated in Table 1 are not sharply separated, but are linked together in a virtually seamless continuum.

5

SCHOENBERG

Piano Piece, Opus 33a (1929)

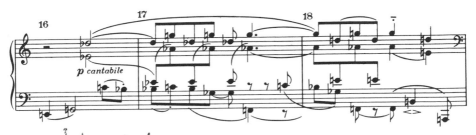

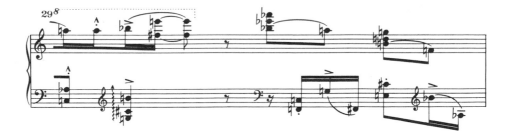

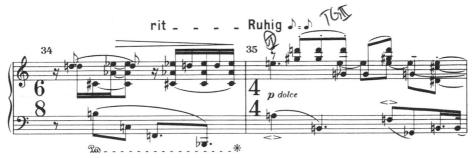

ANALYTICAL COMMENTS

Op. 33a is a twelve-tone piece, composed after Schoenberg had developed all the essential resources of his new compositional technique. Throughout the piece he limits himself to combinatorial pairs for simultaneously sounding row forms.[1] The untransposed principal form, P-0, is combinatorial with I-5, as is—necessarily—its retrograde (R-0) with RI-5. These four forms provide the basic row group for the composition:

EXAMPLE 1

Table 1 gives the distribution of rows grouped according to the principal sections. (Row forms connected by slashes occur simultaneously, the first played by the right hand, the second by the left; rows listed singly are distributed between both hands.) Since beginnings and endings of rows normally coincide with beginnings and endings of phrases, row structure and form are closely aligned at this level.

TABLE 1

Section I

1. mm. 1–9   P-0—RI-5—RI-5 / R-0—P-0—RI-5—P-0 / I-5
2. mm. 10–13   P-0 / I-5—RI-5 / R-0—I-5 / P-0
3. mm. 14–22   P-0 / I-5—R-0(1–10) / RI-5(1–10)—P-0(7–12) / I-5 (7–11)
4. mm. 23–27.3   P-0 / I-5—P-0 / I-5—R-0

Section II

1. mm. 27.4–32.1   P-2(1–6) / I-7(1–6)—I-0(1–6) / P-7(1–6)— P-2 / I-7—I-0/P-7—I-0 / P-7—R-7 / RI-0

Section III

1. mm. 32.3–34   P-0 / I-5—RI-5 / R-0
2. mm. 35–36   R-0 / RI-5
3. mm. 37–40   P-0—RI-5—I-5—R-0—P-0 / I-5

---

1.   See pp. 195–97 of Morgan, *Twentieth-Century Music* (New York, 1991), for a discussion of "combinatoriality" in reference to this piece.

All paired rows are combinatorial, avoiding pitch duplication between corresponding hexachords, and single rows appear in consecutive combinatorial pairs; i.e., the second hexachord of the first row is combinatorial with the first of the second. Thus P-0 is followed by RI-5 in mm. 1–2, 6–7, 32–33, and 37, and I-5 is followed by R-0 in m. 38. (The single statement of R-0 in m. 27 is an exception, though it is combinatorial with the previous I-5). These consecutive pairs appear only in the first and third sections, another correspondence between row structure and form.

Of several inconsistencies within individual rows, two are probably printer's errors: A instead of A♭ in P-0 in m. 22 (right hand), and B instead of B♭ in RI-5 in m. 35 (left hand). In addition, several rows are incomplete: both rows in the R-0 / RI-5 pair in mm. 19–20 lack their last two pitches (B♭–F and E♭–A♭), and the following P-0 / I-5 pair has only second hexachords, which are, however, combinatorial with the final (incomplete) hexachords of the previous pair. And I-5 in mm. 21–22 is itself incomplete, lacking a final A.

The most dramatic departure from normal twelve-tone procedures occurs in the more developmental middle section, where the first simultaneous pair, P-2 / I-7, is interrupted after the first hexachord by I-0 / P-7 (m. 28.1). The latter pair is in turn interrupted by the return of P-2 / I-7, now complete, followed by the return of I-0 / P-7, also complete.

At several points the order of adjacent pitches is reversed. The reasons—having to do with motivic associations—are usually evident. The most extreme instance occurs in mm. 12–13 in the left hand, where the order of P-0 is freely permuted within the three well-articulated tetrachords. This more "chordal" conception prepares for the contrasting material at m. 14, where (after presentation in correct order) the pitches are freely repeated.

A distinctive feature of this row is its two initial perfect fifths. Since musical gestures tend to correspond to row forms, most of the gestures in this piece either begin or end with fifths. Moreover, since P forms are normally combined with combinatorial I forms, and R forms with combinatorial RI forms, the fifths in simultaneous pairs usually appear together, and since the row is combinatorial at I-5 (a perfect fifth lower), these fifths are themselves fifth-related.

Fifths are especially exposed in mm. 23–25, which contain the cadential gesture for the first main section (mm. 23–24) and the first measure of a transitional segment (mm. 25–27) leading to the second section. (In fact, the previously mentioned missing fifths in m. 20 and the missing A in the left hand at m. 22—which would form a fifth with the right-hand E at m. 23.1—were perhaps omitted to save the interval for this cadence.) The only two transpositions of the basic row group used, by a perfect fifth and major second (i.e., two perfect fifths), also reflect this property of the row.

More detailed aspects of the form can be seen, for example, in the opening "pre-thematic" chordal gesture, which functions as a "motto" and returns to announce two later segments (mm. 10, 28). The first thematic segment, mm. 3–7, comprises three one-measure units, in which the initial rising gesture to F^4 (m. 3.2) is carried by successive major sevenths onward to E^5 (m. 4.2) and $D\#^6$ (m. 5.3, left hand), followed by a falling motion (mm. 6–7). The complete statement mirrors the contour of the motto (as do a number of subsequent passages and, to some extent, the composition as a whole). The return of the motto in mm. 10–11 is developed rhythmically and texturally, and is followed in mm. 12–13 by a highly compressed version of the thematic statement of mm. 3–7 that functions as a transition.

The slower and more lyrical contrasting theme at mm. 14ff., marked *cantabile,* has longer note values, many more repeated notes, and a slower "harmonic rhythm"—i.e., the rows are used up more slowly (a single pair of rows lasts five measures) and grouped internally by six notes instead of four. This music is interrupted in mm. 19–20 by the return of material similar to mm. 8–9, which had also been interruptive, and returns in mm. 21–22 to lead to the cadential music of mm. 23–24. (The transitional mm. 25–27 are also closely related to these interruptive segments.)

The strongly contrasting character of mm. 14ff. suggests that the piece might be viewed as a sonata form: principal theme (mm. 1–13, 10–13 being transitional), subordinate theme (mm. 14–27, with 23–27 closing and transitional), development (mm. 27–32), and recapitulation (principal theme, mm. 32–33; transition, 34; subordinate theme, 35–36; closing, 37–40). Only the larger outlines of this parsing are supported by the row structure, however, since no transposition (i.e., "modulation") occurs in the exposition. Moreover, though the recapitulation resembles the exposition in being more continuous than the development (whose fragmentary and repetitive character conforms to convention), its opening segment (mm. 32–33) provides the most compressed, rhythmically active, and registrally extended version of the original material, and (despite the soft dynamic level) further intensifies the development process in an essentially unbroken gesture. (The motto, already compressed almost beyond recognition at the beginning of the development, is omitted entirely in the reprise.)

Certain aspects of the contrasting material at m. 14 are anticipated in the interruption at mm. 8–9 (notably the predominance of repeated-note figures), a relation highlighted when the similarly interruptive music of mm. 19–20 is immediately followed by the new theme in mm. 21–22. The development is concerned exclusively with material derived from the three interruptive segments and thus relates equally to both themes of the exposition. In the recapitulation the interruptive material is avoided entirely, so that the two themes, now integrated, join in a single arc projecting the contour of the motto (mm. 32–35).

6

CHARLES IVES (1874–1954)
General William Booth Enters into Heaven
(1914)

*Both small and large notes in voice part are sung if there is a chorus.

Oct's 8va basso ad lib.

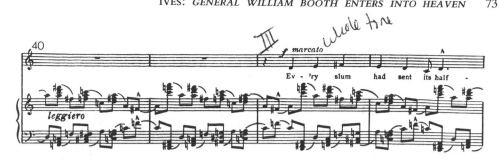

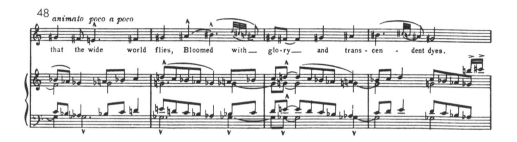

Booth led boldly with his big brass drum—
(Are you washed in the blood of the Lamb?)
Saints smiled gravely and they said: "He's come."
(Are you washed in the blood of the Lamb?)
Walking lepers followed rank on rank,
Lurching bravoes from the ditches dank,
Drabs from alleyways and drug fiends pale
Minds still passion-ridden, soul powers frail:
Vermin-eaten saints with moldy breath,
Unwashed legions with the ways of Death—
(Are you washed in the blood of the Lamb?)

Every slum had sent its half-a-score
The round world over. (Booth had groaned for more.)
Every banner that the wide world flies,
Bloomed with glory and transcendent dyes.
Big-voiced lassies made their banjos bang,
Tranced, fanatical they shrieked and sang—
"Are you washed in the blood of the Lamb?"
Hallelujah! It was queer to see
Bull-necked convicts with that land make free.
Loons with trumpets blowed a blare, blare, blare

goes to simpler music

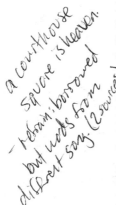

— a courthouse square is heaven.
— refrain borrowed but words from different song (2 sources)

Booth led boldly with his big brass drum—
(Are you washed in the blood of the Lamb?)
Saints smiled gravely and they said: "He's come."
(Are you washed in the blood of the Lamb?)
Walking lepers followed rank on rank,
Lurching bravoes from the ditches dank,
Drabs from alleyways and drug fiends pale
Minds still passion-ridden, soul powers frail:
Vermin-eaten saints with moldy breath,
Unwashed legions with the ways of Death—
(Are you washed in the blood of the Lamb?)

Every slum had sent its half-a-score
The round world over. (Booth had groaned for more.)
Every banner that the wide world flies,
Bloomed with glory and transcendent dyes.
Big-voiced lassies made their banjos bang,
Tranced, fanatical they shrieked and sang—
"Are you washed in the blood of the Lamb?"
Hallelujah! It was queer to see
Bull-necked convicts with that land make free.
Loons with trumpets blowed a blare, blare, blare

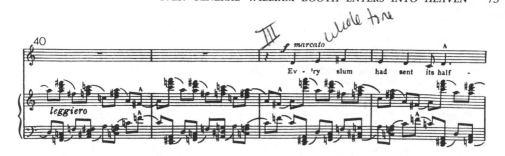

On, on upward through the golden air!
(Are you washed in the blood of the Lamb?)

Jesus came from [out] the courthouse door,
Stretched his hands above the passing poor.
Booth saw not, but led his queer ones there
Round and round the mighty courthouse square.
Yet! in an instant all that blear review
Marched on spotless, clad in raiment new.
⌣ The lame were straightened, withered limbs uncurled
And blind eyes opened on a new, sweet world.
Are you washed in the blood of the Lamb?

ANALYTICAL COMMENTS

Ives's setting of Vachel Lindsay's poem about William Booth, the founder
and first commanding general of the Salvation Army, juxtaposes technical
complexity and expressive immediacy in a manner typical of the composer.
The text, which portrays Booth leading his motley crew of social and physical misfits into heaven, where they are transformed and made whole through
the appearance of Jesus, provides an ideal vehicle for Ives to draw upon his
wide-ranging musical sources.

   There are frequent suggestions of march music, underscored at the opening by the simulated bass drum of the low recurring figures of the piano
accompaniment. Fragments from the refrain of the hymn tune *Cleansing
Fountain*, distorted yet easily recognizable, appear throughout in conjunction with the textual refrain "Are you washed in the blood of the Lamb?,"
itself borrowed by Lindsay from a well-known Salvation Army hymn (mm.
5–8, 15–19, 34–38, 58–60, 76–81). These lead to a complete statement of
the hymn at m. 98, the refrain appearing in a different key (E major instead
of C) and at a slower tempo. Additional quoted materials include the minstrel tune *Oh, Dem Golden Slippers!*, introduced in the top voice of the piano
in mm. 52–55 (accompanying a reference to "banjos"), and the bugle call
Reveille in mm. 70–73 (accompanying "trumpets") and more vaguely in
95–97 (accompanying "marched").

   The overall organization of the song is cumulative. Despite its essentially
ongoing and unbroken character, the music can be divided into six sections,
each marked by a shift of focus in the text:

Section	I	II	III	IV	V	VI
mm.	1–20	21–39	40–60	61–81	82–90	91–113

All but one of these segments are approximately twenty measures in length
and end with statements of the refrain. The exception is the next-to-last
section (V), a scene of transfiguration at a slower tempo, which is abruptly
interrupted by the return of the opening accompanimental figure, followed

7

BÉLA BARTÓK (1881–1945)
Bluebeard's Castle (1911), opening segment

(A small iron door opens at the top of the stairs and in the blinding light two figures are silhouetted, Bluebeard and Judith)

7

BÉLA BARTÓK (1881–1945)
Bluebeard's Castle (1911), opening segment

monization of the tune at the end of the song, culminating in the completely triadic presentation of the last phrase of the refrain to appear (m. 109). The diatonicism of this pure version is prepared not only by the almost functionally normal bass progression of the preceding hymn setting (mm. 98ff.) but also by the similarly diatonic music for the transfiguration (mm. 82ff.). The latter offers a moment of striking relaxation as Booth's followers march "round and round" the square, their motion mirrored by the circling vocal line, which keeps going over the same three pitches, C–B♭–A♭. (This is itself prepared through the circling dissolution of the melody of the preceding refrain, mm. 79–81.) The somewhat veiled anticipation of the complete hymn tune in the piano left hand at the transfiguration, mm. 82–88, is not allowed to complete itself, but similarly spins around these same three pitches until interrupted by the return of the opening accompaniment.

The long-awaited appearance of the complete hymn tune forms the principal climax of the song, breaking out in the final section with such intensity as to recall the fervor and enthusiasm of a revival meeting. The impression was no doubt intended, as Ives witnessed many such meetings as a child and was deeply impressed by them. (One of his instrumental pieces, the third movement of the Second Violin Sonata, carries the title "The Revival.")

by the final, complete hymn statement. Although the content of the six sections varies, thematic cohesion is achieved through a number of recurring elements, the most important being the hymn refrain.

Ives links the quoted materials in the song through various associations. The opening vocal phrase (mm. 3–4), which like the refrain appears several times throughout, begins with a rising triadic motion that, though minor rather than major, closely resembles the opening of the hymn (compare the setting of "Booth led boldly" and "Are you washed" in mm. 3–5). The quotations from *Reveille* and the minstrel song also relate to the hymn, the latter through the rising scalar third that introduces the last phrase before the refrain (mm. 103.4–104.1, with the words "opened on"), the former through its similar triadic arpeggiations (this less apparent connection is underlined when the bugle tune leads into the complete statement of the hymn, mm. 95–99).

On a more abstract level, the predominantly whole-tone vocal line of much of the extended description of Booth's followers in mm. 25–57 (purely whole-tone in mm. 42–51) is tied to their transfiguration as Jesus appears (mm. 82ff.). Although the latter section is almost entirely diatonic and triadic, the voice consistently colors the A♭-major tonality with G♭, ending each of its three phrases on this pitch, thus producing the whole-tone segment C–B♭–A♭–G♭. (The last of these G♭'s, in m. 91, spelled F♯, accompanies the text's "Yet!," denoting a shift that brings about the return of the opening drum figure.)

Although unambiguously triadic harmony becomes prominent only near the end of the song, especially in mm. 82ff. and 109, triadic key centers are strongly suggested by both the opening vocal phrase (B minor, mm. 3–4, supported to some degree by the accompaniment, which contains a B-minor triad) and the quoted refrain that immediately follows (C major, mm. 5–8, also partly supported in the accompaniment, containing a C-major triad). As noted, both of these phrases recur several times. But whereas the opening vocal phrase consistently returns to its original B-minor tonal orientation (mm. 3–4, 13–15, 21–24 [B major], 74–75, 91–97 [accompaniment only]), the refrain changes focus: from C (mm. 5–8) to E (15–19), C♯ minor (34–38), G (58–60), and E♭ (76–81). The complete hymn tune then returns to the first two keys associated with the refrain: C major (the hymn proper, mm. 98–105) and E major (the refrain, mm. 106–10).

The first four key changes associated with the refrain are linked to a gradual intensification of the music, which reaches a plateau with the repeated "Hallelujah"s of mm. 61–65. With each change the top note of the triadic figure moves higher: from G^4 (mm. 5–8) to B^4 (15–19), $C\sharp^5$ (34–38), and D^5 (58–60)—the last, decorated by an upper neighbor E^5, is also maintained through the "Hallelujah" segment. Increasing rhythmic excitement, especially in the accompaniment, accompanies this larger development.

As often in compositions dominated by a single borrowed tune, Ives creates a sort of climax in reverse by gradually moving toward a simple har-

On, on upward through the golden air!
(Are you washed in the blood of the Lamb?)

Jesus came from [out] the courthouse door,
Stretched his hands above the passing poor.
Booth saw not, but led his queer ones there
Round and round the mighty courthouse square.
Yet! in an instant all that blear review
Marched on spotless, clad in raiment new.
⌣ The lame were straightened, withered limbs uncurled
And blind eyes opened on a new, sweet world.
Are you washed in the blood of the Lamb?

ANALYTICAL COMMENTS

Ives's setting of Vachel Lindsay's poem about William Booth, the founder
and first commanding general of the Salvation Army, juxtaposes technical
complexity and expressive immediacy in a manner typical of the composer.
The text, which portrays Booth leading his motley crew of social and physical misfits into heaven, where they are transformed and made whole through
the appearance of Jesus, provides an ideal vehicle for Ives to draw upon his
wide-ranging musical sources.

There are frequent suggestions of march music, underscored at the opening by the simulated bass drum of the low recurring figures of the piano
accompaniment. Fragments from the refrain of the hymn tune *Cleansing
Fountain,* distorted yet easily recognizable, appear throughout in conjunction with the textual refrain "Are you washed in the blood of the Lamb?,"
itself borrowed by Lindsay from a well-known Salvation Army hymn (mm.
5–8, 15–19, 34–38, 58–60, 76–81). These lead to a complete statement of
the hymn at m. 98, the refrain appearing in a different key (E major instead
of C) and at a slower tempo. Additional quoted materials include the minstrel tune *Oh, Dem Golden Slippers!,* introduced in the top voice of the piano
in mm. 52–55 (accompanying a reference to "banjos"), and the bugle call
Reveille in mm. 70–73 (accompanying "trumpets") and more vaguely in
95–97 (accompanying "marched").

The overall organization of the song is cumulative. Despite its essentially
ongoing and unbroken character, the music can be divided into six sections,
each marked by a shift of focus in the text:

Section	I	II	III	IV	V	VI
mm.	1–20	21–39	40–60	61–81	82–90	91–113

All but one of these segments are approximately twenty measures in length
and end with statements of the refrain. The exception is the next-to-last
section (V), a scene of transfiguration at a slower tempo, which is abruptly
interrupted by the return of the opening accompanimental figure, followed

(Bluebeard, at the bottom of the steps, turns and looks at Judith, who has stopped half-way down. A ray of light from the open door shines on both of them.)

ANALYTICAL COMMENTS

Bluebeard's Castle is the first work in which Bartók achieved a complete synthesis of folk-music elements within his personal idiom. Despite many traditional features, the opera's modernity is evident in the essentially symphonic one-act structure, without arias or other set numbers, and in the almost exclusively psychological nature of the drama, which is without real action, everything being internalized. Though the two characters converse throughout in dialogue form, they achieve no significant contact. Indeed, the focus is really on the castle more than the characters within it, as expressed in a single, obsessive image: the locked doors concealing the castle's—and Bluebeard's—past.

The plot is based on the well-known legend of Duke Bluebeard, said to have murdered each of his wives before taking the next. In Béla Balázs's libretto, however, the wives represent but one layer of the protagonist's hidden life. Though apparently still alive, their physical status remains uncertain, even unimportant; what matters is not their death but the death of Bluebeard's love for them.

The story is simply told: Judith, Bluebeard's new wife, discovers seven locked doors and convinces her husband to give her the keys to the doors, one by one, so she can discover what lies behind them. The musical structure, though ultimately continuous, contains seven brief "scenes," each associated with the opening of a door, framed by an extended introductory section and a brief closing one. The doors open to reveal both Bluebeard's magnificent possessions (treasure room, gardens, and extensive lands) and the cruelty and thirst for domination that made possible their acquisition (torture chamber, armory, and a lake filled with the tears of those who suffered for his gain). The last door reveals the previous wives, whom Judith joins as the opera closes.

The allegorical nature of the story suggests several interpretations, the most obvious being that the castle represents Bluebeard's soul, coveted by Judith but attainable only at the expense of innocence and trust. So viewed, the opera portrays the illusory nature of perfect love—the ultimate impossibility of absolute belief and commitment between two separate beings. Another reading might draw upon sexual stereotypes: the powerful, dominating, and evil male versus the possessive, intrusive, and untrusting female. On the broadest level the story offers a Faustian parable of human ambition—the desire to gain knowledge, master nature, and unlock the mysteries of life.

This excerpt represents the first half of the opera's opening section, introducing the two characters and ending with Judith's determination to explore the castle. (In the second half of the introduction Judith discovers the seven doors and attains the first key.) The excerpt is divided into three musical-dramatic units, differentiated by three closely related key areas, F♯, D♯, and C♯, with F♯ providing the overall focus. During the first unit (to m. 93) Bluebeard and Judith enter the castle and descend the staircase into the main hall; in the second (mm. 93–143) Judith comments on the castle's darkness; and in the third (mm. 144–253) she expresses her decision to remain and brighten the castle.

The opera opens with four four-measure phrases (the first three articulated by fermatas on their final notes), derived from a single pentatonic scale (Example 1a):

EXAMPLE 1

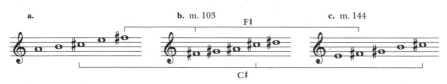

F♯ initiates the first two phrases and closes the final one, and is further supported by the fifth-related C♯ closing the first and third phrases. The cadential F♯ of the final phrase (m. 16), overlapping with a new segment, is immediately associated with C♮ rather than C♯, the chromatic pitch appearing as part of a neighbor-note motive that plays an important role throughout the first unit (it is especially prominent in m. 53, where it punctuates Bluebeard's arrival at the bottom of the staircase).

The F♯–C tritone is central to the overall tonal organization, as are tritone relationships in general. It is originally generated through one of the work's primary strategies, the alteration of pentatonic material through chromatic inflection. Throughout the score, especially in the voice parts, short, simply inflected phrases that are basically pentatonic in derivation (the fruit of Bartók's folk-song explorations) preponderate, underscoring the primeval, quasi-mythical nature of the dramatic material.

The importance of F♯ is confirmed later in the unit. An F♯-minor triad supplies the cadential goal of the first larger phrase (m. 29), accompanying Bluebeard's first words; F♯ reappears in the bass in m. 44, as Bluebeard asks Judith if she regrets coming (here supporting a chord that includes the tritone-related C♮); and it appears again in m. 57, as Bluebeard asks Judith if she will remain, and in m. 73, the goal of three V–I progressions (very much the exception in the opera, and here obscured by the voice). Finally, F♯ returns at the end of the first unit, from m. 91, where it begins to reassert itself in preparation for the second unit, gradually formed in mm. 93–103.

The end of the first unit is defined dramatically by the closing of the entrance door in m. 93, symbolizing Judith's decision to remain, and musically by the gradual transformation of the two-note motive prominent in the orchestral top voice from m. 82 (first introduced in m. 20) into the low ostinato figure that marks the beginning of the new unit. This second unit, like the first, begins with pure pentatonic material, again containing both F♯ and C♯ but derived from a different scale (Example 1b). Once under way, however, the tonal focus shifts from F♯ to D♯ (m. 103). As in the previous unit, chromatic elements are progressively introduced into the pentatonic opening, here linked with Judith's increasing anxiety over the castle's gloomy appearance.

A tritone-related A♮, corresponding to C♮ in the first section, appears in the orchestra in m. 119, then in the voice in m. 123 and, more emphatically, in m. 128, where Judith makes her first physical contact with the castle, remarking that the walls are wet. The A's in m. 128 are heard in conjunction with a simultaneous orchestral A-G♯ (derived from the chromatic neighbor motive in m. 16), associated throughout with the dramatic motive of blood. After a temporary move back to F♯, the tonal focus shifts to a sustained G-major triad in m. 136 (linked with a prominent tritone-related C♯ in the voice that is held over from the previous F♯ complex), marking the close of the second unit.

C♯ becomes the principal focus of the third unit in m. 144, supported by a new ostinato derived from yet a third pentatonic scale containing F♯ and C♯ (Example 1c). Here the pentatonic basis is more quickly compromised, as Judith becomes increasingly agitated. In m. 151 the tritone-related G♮ appears, to which the bass responds with chromatic movement filling in the third C^2-E^2 before returning to C♯ in m. 168. Judith's agitation is also projected by the vocal line, rising to three increasingly higher points: E^5 (m. 169), G^5 (195), $G\sharp^5$ (213). The first two of these follow and precede a return to C♯ in the orchestral bass (mm. 168, 203), while the third, mirroring the hopelessness of her situation, quickly gives way to an abrupt dissolution, returning to the ostinato figure at m. 221, now significantly altered to emphasize a tritone (F-B) rather than a perfect fourth. At m. 238 the ostinato is again altered, reaching a C bass pedal at m. 244 and sustained almost to the close of the excerpt. Over this ostinato three fragmentary references to the opening pentatonic music appear in the middle voice, each closing on F♯ (thus bringing back the original F♯-C tritone relationship).

Though F♯ is rather weakly established here (giving way completely in the last measure of the excerpt), its return is significant in the context of the return of the entire opening pentatonic music, untransposed, near the beginning of the second part of the introductory section. (F♯ is also the tonal center of the scene associated with the first door.) When, at the close of the opera, the opening pentatonic music is recapitulated once more, an F♯ focus is established for the whole.

8

BARTÓK

from *Mikrokosmos*, Vol. VI (1939)

    a. No. 148, *Six Dances in Bulgarian Rhythm*, No. 1

b. No. 140, *Free Variations*

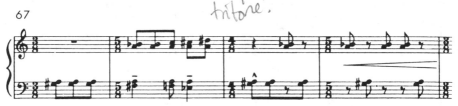

c. No. 144, *Minor Seconds, Major Sevenths*

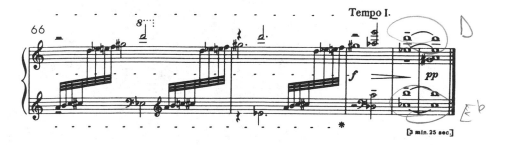

[3 min. 25 sec.]

ANALYTICAL COMMENTS

These three pieces, from the sixth and final volume of the didactic piano collection *Mikrokosmos,* illustrate in miniature various features of Bartók's mature compositional technique. For analytic purposes, they are presented here in order of increasingly chromatic pitch language, (Nos. 148/1, 140, 144) rather than in their published order.

All of the *Six Dances in Bulgarian Rhythm* feature a combination of unequal groupings of eighth notes borrowed from Bulgarian folk music, though the melodic materials are Bartók's own. Despite frequent syncopations, the underlying $4+2+3$ grouping of this first dance is usually clear. The piece begins and ends unambiguously on E and demonstrates a type of diatonically derived—yet not traditionally major-minor—tonality common in Bartók. Taken separately, both melody and accompaniment are largely diatonic, yet constant clashes produce what Bartók called "polymodal chromaticism."[1] At the opening, for example, the right hand is major and the left is Phrygian; these are reversed when the principal melody begins in m. 4. The resulting chromatic clashes, especially between D and D♯ (and to a lesser extent F and F♯), persist throughout.

The tonic E, defined mainly by reiteration, appears as the bass of the ostinato-like accompaniment and as the principal melodic tone. Example 1 sketches the main tonal motion of the first section, mm. 1–21. The melody of the first phrase (mm. 4–8) outlines E^5-A^4-E^4 and thus provides a modal (subdominant) inflection rather than a traditional dominant one, that underlies the overall shape of the piece. When the melody repeats (m. 9), it again descends to A^4, but then moves upward from G^4 to C^5 to G^5, inverting the previous falling pattern and suggesting a shift of tonal focus. The bass responds by moving to C (m. 14), supporting a Lydian scale that retains F♯ from the previous segment, which had already been associated with C in m. 13. (The bass D♭ in m. 14 brings back the Phrygian second.) At mm. 14–17 a new version of the melody appears, now expanded to descend through two fifths, then repeated in mm. 18–21 as the bass moves another third to A. With the arrival of B^3 at m. 21.3 (related by tritone rather than perfect fifth to the previous F^4), the melody dissolves into a transitional section.

EXAMPLE 1

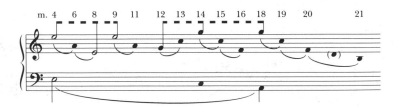

1.   See Béla Bartók, *Essays,* ed. Benjamin Suchoff (New York, 1976), especially pp. 364–71 and 376–83.

Though the harmony in this first section is largely nonfunctional and nontriadic, there are unmistakable references to triadic tonality that have later repercussions. The F♯–D♯ on the final three eighths in each of the first thirteen measures suggest V (or VII). Although initially combined with F and D♮, weakening their functional meaning, they later appear with B, producing complete dominants at mm. 7, 10-12, and 13, resolving deceptively to VI at m. 14.

Later these veiled functional and triadic implications become more emphatic. At m. 32, following the transitional section, the melody from m. 4 returns with a more triadic orientation. As before, it descends to A^4, but then ascends to E^5 and A^5, suggesting a tonal focus on A rather than E, which the accompaniment supports with a pure A-major triad at m. 37.1. A-major triads return at mm. 38.1 and 39.1 (the first with added A♯, the second with G♮). M. 39 initiates an extended progression by fifths, first upward, A-E (m. 40.1)-B (m. 42.1), then back down, E (m. 42.4)-A (m. 43.2)-D (m. 43.4)-G (m. 44.2)-C (m. 46.1).

The return to E is also supported by a major triad (m. 49), though approached not by fifth but by a stepwise bass (bringing back the Phrygian seventh from the opening), and E is confirmed at m. 53, again with triadic support. Finally, E is emphasized in a pure Phrygian passage (mm. 56–60), the beginning notes of whose melodic sequences—A-G-F-E—outline the critical A-E relationship that underlies the entire piece: the first section moves from E to A (Example 1), A supplies the (partly unstable) tonal focus for the extended central portion (mm. 16–39, encompassing the melodic repeat from m. 32), and the circle-of-fifths progression brings the motion back to E at m. 49, overlapping with the beginning of the final section (m. 45). The two final chords summarize this motion.

The *Free Variations* employs an "artificial" scale, the octatonic (alternating half and whole steps), and emphasizes symmetrical constructions, which reflect the nature of that scale.[2] Of its five main sections, all but one are variations on the same idea (two additional passages, mm. 24–33 and 44–51, are transitional):

Variation I	Variation II	Variation III	*B*	Variation IV
mm. 1–12	13–24	34–44	52–64	65–82

The principal phrase of the first variation features a pedal A combined with an octatonic descent: (A)-G♯-F♯-F-E♭-D. Each subphrase of the three-

2.   For an introduction to pitch symmetry with particular reference to Bartók's music, see Elliott Antokoletz, *The Music of Béla Bartók* (Berkeley and Los Angeles, 1984), especially pp. 67–78. This composition, as well as *Minor Seconds, Major Sevenths,* has been analyzed in a somewhat related manner by Ivan Waldbauer in "Interplay of Tonality and Nontonal Constructs in Three Pieces from the *Mikrokosmos* of Bartók," included in Anne Dhu Shapiro, ed., *Music and Context: Essays for John M. Ward* (Cambridge, Mass., 1985), pp. 418–40.

part "sentence" structure $(2+2+3)$ carries the descent down, the last sub-phrase cadencing on the fifth D-A (m. 7). This interval, suggesting a focus on D, is then composed out as a new pitch—B♭—in the right hand (to this point accompanimental) and generates a chromatic motion filling A^3-D^4, while the left hand (with A now in the bass, weakening the D focus) fills D^3-A^3 (mm. 10ff.).

The second variation inverts the first, the octatonic scale rising in the right hand to A-E in m. 19 (suggesting A centricity), followed by chromatic extensions in the left. These extensions are more complex than before, and the left-hand pedal is now mobile, moving to C (m. 20) and C♯ (mm. 21–23) and holding these pitches through the first transition section (mm. 24–33).

In Variation III the idea of inverted imitation comes more to the fore, having been anticipated in the second variation's relation to the first (and in the abortive attempt of the left hand to start downward in m. 14). Chromatic elements now appear within a rhythmically compressed version of the octatonic materials; and whereas the right hand rises a fifth, the left stops at D♯ (instead of D♮). D♯ and E, defining the section's total compass, are retained as the outer limits of the transition section (mm. 44–50), transferred to a lower octave and inverted. Compensating for the absence of cadence in Variation III, this transition provides a dissolution in preparation for the *B* section.

The final variation (beginning at m. 65) presents the idea of inversional imitation in its strictest form. The first section's phrase structure (slightly altered to accommodate the imitative idea) and pitch material return in the left hand, with the right hand imitating in inversion one measure later, both hands cadencing on perfect fifths (simultaneously at m. 72.2). Again the cadence is followed by chromatic extensions, now in a long, coda-like passage (mm. 73ff.) that alternates A and D tonal focuses in strict imitation. Although this passage seems to confirm a more traditionally tonal D, with A as its dominant, Bartók ultimately opts for a symmetrical ending, bringing D up chromatically (mm. 77–82) to close on A, the symmetrical center of the two octatonic collections the piece employs.

To achieve symmetry around A, two such collections are required, since no single octatonic scale is inversionally symmetrical around a single pitch. Example 2 illustrates this point: whereas the two octatonic configurations in 2a (used by Bartók) radiate symmetrically outward from A, the single scale in 2b is asymmetrical around A.

The contrasting *B* section, on the other hand, *is* derived from a single octatonic scale. (The only exceptions are the left-hand D^6's, mm. 56–57.) This section exploits a salient octatonic property, transpositional equivalency at the tritone: the right hand of mm. 52–57, beginning on F♯ (spelled G♭) and ending on C (a tritone away), is repeated in mm. 58–64 exactly transposed, beginning on C and ending on F♯, remaining within the same octatonic collection. (The left-hand accompaniment is similarly transposed to the right hand, C in m. 52 becoming F♯ in m. 58, etc.) Thus section *B*,

EXAMPLE 2

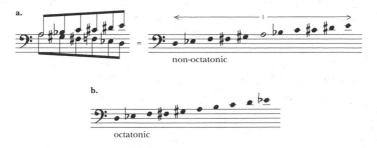

non-octatonic

octatonic

while sharing certain similarities with the variations, is set apart by its octa-
tonicism as well as its slower tempo, new texture, and more lyrical character.

Inversional symmetrical construction framed in a more chromatic environment figures even more prominently in *Minor Seconds, Major Sevenths*. The
main idea is presented in mm. 1–2: two minor seconds separated by a half
step (filling G^4-$B\flat^4$) radiate outward symmetrically, first by a minor second
(to $F\sharp^4$-B^4), then by a minor third (to $E\flat^4$-D^5). The total configuration spans
$E\flat^4$-D^5, with A^4-$G\sharp^4$ as the axis of symmetry (Example 3a).

EXAMPLE 3

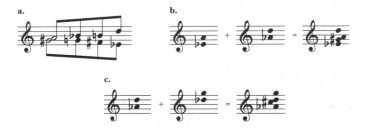

    The $E\flat$-D goal is underlined by symmetrically placed octave repetitions
(m. 2.3). The opening configuration (mm. 1-2) appears throughout mm.
1–16, first untransposed (mm. 1–8), then transposed up a perfect fourth
(mm. 8–16, developing further upward in mm. 13–14 but returning to $A\flat$-
G at m. 16). It reappears at the original pitch in the final section (mm. 61–
70). The piece thus establishes a "tonal region" (nonfunctional and nontriadic), transposes it, and, after a departure, returns to it.
    The transposition level of a fourth is itself derived from mm. 1–2, which
emphasize the fourth F♯-B motivically (it sounds three times in m. 1). The
basic configuration can also be generated by the perfect-fourth transposition
of the tritone $E\flat$-A (Example 3b), and an additional such transposition produces the $A\flat$-G complex of mm. 8–16 (Example 3c). The fourth is also

emphasized melodically when the top-voice D^6 is elaborated by G^6 (mm. 4.2–5.1), an idea that evolves into the pentatonic melody of mm. 6.4–8.1, which elaborates the descending-fourth sequence C^6-G^5-D^5. The last fourth, G–D (also outlined in the upper voice of the left hand in inversion, mm. 6.4–8.1), provides the cadence, bringing back the fourth from mm. 4–5 and preparing the transposition to G in mm. 8–9. This pentatonic melody reappears in mm. 55–60, leading back to the return of the opening material.

Though the material of the contrasting middle section (mm. 18–55) changes more quickly, it resembles the outer ones in that it is generated by outward radiations from minor-second axes of symmetry. In mm. 18–28 the center is F^4-$F\sharp^4$, expanding first to C^4-B^4 (m. 21), then $B\flat^3$-$F\sharp^5$ (m. 25). The first expansion ends with the configuration of Example 3a, transposed down by a minor third, while the second generates a new goal sonority, $B\flat$-F-$F\sharp$-$C\sharp$. But when that sonority is itself transposed down a minor third (m. 29), the result is a chord also closely related to the configuration of Example 3a, which initiates a brief, registrally developed reference to the original idea in mm. 37–38.

A segment similar to the one at m. 18 begins at m. 43, with $A\flat^4$-A^4 as the symmetrical center (the same as mm. 1–8). This segment expands first to $D\flat^4$-E^5 (m. 47), bringing back the sonority of mm. 25–32 a minor third higher, then to A^3-$G\sharp^5$ in m. 51 (duplicating the pitch classes of the symmetrical center). Another brief reference to the original $E\flat$-D configuration follows, first in "arpeggiated" form (m. 52), then reduced to the pitches of Example 3a (mm. 53–54). Although this brings about a return to the original region, the $E\flat$-D configuration here combines climactically with two other symmetrically related major sevenths (introduced at m. 51.3): $F\sharp^2$-$E\sharp^3$ and C^6-B^6. The opening configuration returns in "pure form" in the final section (m. 61), arpeggiated as well as simultaneous—an idea derived from mm. 21–22, where the outer voices of the more figurative echo of the high melodic falling figure from m. 12 duplicate the pitches of the sustained symmetrical chord of m. 21: $F\sharp$-F (m. 21) and C-B (m. 22).

9

IGOR STRAVINSKY (1882–1971)
from *The Rite of Spring* (1913)
a. *Augurs of Spring, Dances of the Young Girls*

Rimsky ↳ beyond recognition

gapped diatonic scale.

b. *Rounds of Spring*

Fl. picc. 1 2
Fl. gr. 1 2
Fl. alto
Ob. 1 2 3 4
C. ing.
Cl. picc. in Mib
Cl. in Sib 1 2
Cl. bas. in Sib 1 2
Fag. 1 2 3
C. Fag. 1 2
Cor. in Fa 1 2 3 4 5 6 7 8
Tr. picc. in Re
Tr. in Do 1 2 3 4
Trbn. 1 2 3
Tbe. 1 2
Timp.
G.C.
Tam-t.
Vl. I
Vl. II
Vle.
Vc.
Cb.
a2
sff
fff
più ff
gliss.
arco
pizz

ANALYTICAL COMMENTS

Like *The Rite of Spring* as a whole, the "Augurs of Spring: Dances of the Young Girls" section draws its principal melodic materials from a small group of pitches within a restricted registral space. These materials are closely related and can almost all be derived from the following diatonic scale segment, encompassing a perfect fourth (Example 1):

EXAMPLE 1

The flute figure introduced three measures before rn 17[1] and continued at rn 17, its transformation from rn 19 to rn 21, the trumpet melody five measures after rn 28, and the ostinato figure heard in almost every measure of this section are all contained within this same tetrachord (0,2,3,5) and its transpositions. And the figure introduced in the horn and flute at rn 25 and expanded in the flute at rn 28, while encompassing a five-note scale segment, emphasizes the same four-note collection (the fifth note, F, being largely ornamental).

The role of the opening sonority as a tonal focus and point of departure for contrasting developments in the first part, "Augurs of Spring,"[2] and its continuing importance in the second part, "Dances of the Young Girls" (beginning at rn 22), are evident from the retention of the ostinato figure of rn 14, consisting of the top three notes of the original chord (B♭-D♭-E♭). This sonority persists unchanged until rn 30 and, after sequential development, continues at a new pitch level from rn 31. Moreover, the music of rn 22 to rn 28, though more diatonic than before, contains five of the seven pitches from the opening sonority, with C♮ replacing C♭ (a substitution already introduced at rn 14 and rn 16).

A second shift of pitch content at rn 28 produces full diatonicism, a collection corresponding to the D♭-major scale; this shift involves the lowering of A to A♭ and G to G♭ and the dropping of E♮ from the previous complex. Since the new scale retains the three notes of the original ostinato, the latter continues to provide a link to the basic sonority. In addition, the recurring bass E♭ (which creates a tonal effect quite different from D♭ major) connects with the bass E♭ of rn 16 to rn 17, as does the return of the cello and bass ostinato from that segment. The principal pitches—B♭-C-D♭-E♭—of the two main melodic components (flutes at rn 28, trumpets four measures later) have also figured prominently before. The D♭ collection persists until rn 30, supplying the basis for the first of two climactic plateaus that punctuate the latter part of the section.

1. In this discussion, the designation rn refers to rehearsal number, as it appears in the score.
2. See Morgan, *Twentieth-Century Music* (New York, 1991), pp. 97–99, for a discussion of this issue.

A brief transition, reintroducing chromaticism, leads from rn 30 to rn 31, where a new diatonic collection, corresponding to the C-major scale (a half-step shift of the entire previous collection), is established. (The A♭ and F♯ in the horn and bassoon merely elaborate the bass note G.) At rn 32 E♭ replaces E♮, after which the pitch content remains unchanged. The music builds quickly to the second major climax, maintained until the close of the section at rn 37, with chromatic scale figurations added for increased intensity from two measures before rn 33. Traditional tonal associations are evoked in this segment, suggesting a dominant configuration in the key of C that implies the possibility of a functionally articulated final cadence: the cello-bass ostinato ends with G, the dominant of C, and the two-chord horn ostinato ends with a G dominant-seventh chord. Moreover, C-major triads have figured prominently during much of the previous music (especially at rn 14 and rn 16), and a C pedal sounds from rn 24 to rn 27.

The resolution, however, proves to be tonally ambiguous. The cadential chord at rn 37, both closing this section and opening the following one ("Ritual of Abduction"), contains a complete C-major chord in the horns, fulfilling the functional implications of their ostinato—but the trumpets add an E♭ dominant-seventh chord. The composite six-note chord brings back all of the notes of the opening configuration except A♭, which is omitted, and C♭, which is replaced by C♮ (by now a familiar substitution).

To summarize, of the two main parts, only the first (rn 13 to rn 22) contains the opening chord, which alternate⌐ with contrasting material in rondo-like fashion *(A-B-A-C-A)*. The more diatonic second part (rn 22 to rn 37), dominated by the horn figure introduced at rn 25, builds to two climactic plateaus, the second providing a final culmination for the entire section. Despite abrupt, typically Stravinskian crosscutting between tonally static segments, a growing sense of momentum is achieved primarily through rhythmic, orchestral, and textural means, directed toward the two climactic plateaus. Thus even the first half is expansive, adding melodic material to the return of the opening chord at rn 15 and rn 19, the latter culminating with the "canon" at rn 21.

The "Rounds of Spring" section differs in being almost entirely diatonic. The section is framed by a brief introduction (rn 48) and its varied return (rn 56), the music of both featuring an E♭ pedal and a "gapped" diatonic scale that sounds almost pentatonic. The melody of the return, based on a slightly different scale (D♮ replacing D♭), is altered in the second half to end on G rather than F (the final note connecting to the prominent F♯ bass that opens the next section). This introductory melody consists of small units that recur in varied form. (For example, when the first unit, m. 1 of rn 48, is immediately repeated, two additional notes plus a grace note are inserted.)

The main body of the section, rn 49 to rn 54, offers an excellent illustration of Stravinsky's practice of alternating polarized formal units. The first segment, rn 49 to rn 50, alternates two such units, each one measure in length, in an irregular pattern of repetitions, 3 + 1 + 2 + 2. Although texturally and orchestrally distinct, the two units are derived from almost identical diatonic scales (G♮ replacing G♭ in the second), and they share an E♭–B♭ pedal bass. The first unit remains unchanged, however, while the second one is compressed one measure before rn 50. At rn 50 the first unit expands and assumes melodic character, taking up the trumpet idea from five measures after rn 28 of "Dances of the Young Girls" (three measures after rn 50, flutes and solo violins, later horns). This material is developed exclusively until rn 52, subjected to typically Stravinskian processes of varied repetition.

At rn 52 the music from rn 49 begins again, but with the first segment compressed to $2 + 1 + 1 + 2$ (rn 52 to rn 53) so that it leads more quickly to the second. The second, now *fortissimo,* builds to a climax of great force, during which chromatic alterations increase the tension.

The sudden interruption at rn 54 cuts off this development in full flight, followed by a sudden, equally unexpected reintroduction of material from "Ritual of Abduction," the section separating "Dances of the Young Girls" from "Rounds of Spring," two measures after rn 54. At rn 56 this material too is abruptly terminated, making way for the return of the introductory section.

missing wit → making you smile
sonata or ritornello form & why?
– French overture → slow, dotted rhythms

STRAVINSKY

Concerto for Piano and Winds (1924), first movement

ANALYTICAL COMMENTS

A product of Stravinsky's 1920s neo-classicism, the Concerto is "internationalist" in orientation, abjuring overt references to the composer's Russian heritage in favor of evocations of eighteenth-century stylistic conventions drawn from the central European tradition. The piano writing is percussive, and the orchestration (without strings except double bass) is clear, dry, and hard-edged.

The first movement combines features of the French overture (slow introduction with dotted rhythm) and Baroque solo concerto. Although Stravinsky considered the work to be "on" rather than "in" A, the overall tonal structure has distinctly traditional traits and is mainly based on major and minor scalar complexes rather than the modal and octatonic ones favored in the composer's earlier works. Characteristic is the juxtaposition of C♯ and C♮, the major and minor thirds within a basically diatonic A context (e.g., mm. 1–2, 33–34), one of numerous chromatic inflections heard throughout the movement and culminating in the final cadenza (mm. 253–312).

Example 1 shows the major formal divisions and tonal areas of the movement (a significant cadence either immediately precedes or overlaps each of the main divisions):

EXAMPLE 1

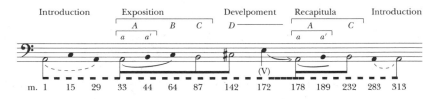

Although tonal areas are defined primarily by emphasis rather than functional progression, functional tonality, like other traditional elements, is frequently evoked: for example, a I-V^7-VI progression in mm. 1–4 and a I-V-I progression in mm. 33–35. Moreover, the cadential points indicated in the diagram contain at least strong hints of V-I (or VII-I) progressions. The return to I at the reprise is articulated by an especially strong bass arrival on E (V) in m. 172 (although, typically for Stravinsky, the resolution is suggested "too soon," at m. 174, four measures before the thematic reprise).

Although all cadential points in Example 1 are sufficiently clear to assure formal definition, m. 87 (and m. 232, the corresponding point in the recapitulation) is somewhat exceptional. Here, though, the cadence on B is relatively weak; the formal division is supported by especially strong thematic, textural, and rhythmic contrast, and B centricity is more emphatically asserted after m. 96.

The larger formal layout consists of an extended Allegro (mm. 33–312) framed by an introduction (mm. 1–32) and its altered reprise (mm. 313–27). Since the first part of the Allegro (encompassing most of mm. 33–141) returns at its end, an arch form results. The introduction, setting the stage for these formal balances, has three phrases beginning with the same thematic idea, mm. 1, 15, and 29 (the last truncated to lead into the Allegro); the middle phrase is distinguished by key (C instead of A), instrumentation, and different continuation.

The movement uses the standard Baroque technique of "spinning out" brief initial figures to create continuously unfolding lines. Although all sections have their own individual motives, these are not strongly differentiated but evolve out of essentially common thematic fabric (reflecting the Baroque principle of "monothematicism"). Thus the main theme of the Allegro stems from the same idea as the introduction: repeated A's and an A–G♯–A neighbor-note figure.

The second subsection of A, m. 44, after restating the head motive of section A, develops in another direction (m. 47), which leads to an apparently new idea in the piano (m. 50). Yet this new idea is derived from the piano, mm. 38.2–39.1, which itself spins out the original neighbor-note figure in an upward direction (already suggested in the piano left hand at mm. 33–34). The woodwind and trumpet figure initiating section B (mm. 64–65) also echoes this idea. Even the new melody in the flute at section C (m. 87), sometimes described as the second theme, is closely related to earlier figures (e.g., as an augmentation of the top voice of the piano at m. 83).

Section D, the development, also has its own motive, a rising syncopated line closing with falling sevenths (mm. 142–45, piano); but this too is evoked earlier, most clearly in the combined horn and clarinet figures of mm. 53–55 (repeated at mm. 84–85, horns only). The persistent presentation of this figure throughout section D (mm. 142, 151, 159, 166, and 168, the first and last time combined with the motive from section C), somewhat in the manner of a fugal exposition, lends this section a strongly contrasting character.

Despite certain similarities to sonata form (see the formal labels in Example 1), this high degree of motivic and figural interpenetration ties the movement more to Baroque than Classical formal precedents. The solo-ensemble relationship of equal and cooperative partners, rather than competitors in a heroic struggle, similarly conforms to Baroque practice.

Though the soloistic passages tend to eschew virtuosic display, they nevertheless enjoy a particularly important formal role. Each of the three principal sections of the exposition ends with a soloistic segment that increases in length: mm. 50–55 (lightly accompanied), 70–87 (mostly unaccompanied), and 110–42 (partly accompanied). All feature similar three-part keyboard textures, reminiscent of Bach inventions (the third introduces more virtuosic solo writing in mm. 110–15, but soon drops it.

After the non-soloistic development, the solo-ensemble alternation returns, sections A and B appearing exactly as before. But section C is altered. After mm. 87–95 are varied and compressed (mm. 232–38, with the "second theme" omitted entirely), mm. 96–108 return exactly (mm. 239–51); but the final, soloistic segment (mm. 110–41) is greatly lengthened and transformed, the piano assuming a more virtuosic character (based on the texture of mm. 110–15) and the three-part texture disappearing entirely. This cadenza-like passage provides a dramatic preparation for the return of the introduction (notable for the supposedly "unemotional" Stravinsky), which, moreover, reappears not in its original form, according to Baroque conventions, but in a fuller, cadential version complete with piano arpeggiations that offers a sort of final peroration. The introductions's *Largo* is prepared by the surprising change of tempo at m. 283: though marked *Più mosso,* it sounds slower because of the sudden absence of sixteenth notes.

The movement contains rhythmic and melodic traits long associated with Stravinsky, here adjusted to conform to the neo-classical stylistic surroundings. The juxtaposition of ostinato-like patterns of different length, for example, is recast within more classically derived contrapuntal textures: e.g., the piano's principal thematic statement at m. 33, where the right-hand repetition in m. 36 begins a beat later than that in the left hand, bringing the two parts out of phase. Especially rich in this regard is the passage from mm. 159–72 of the development, during which simultaneous thematic and igurational ideas (varied by transposition, fragmentation, etc.) are juxtaposed in ever-changing combinations.

11

ANTON WEBERN (1883–1945)

a. Song, Opus 3, No. 1 (1909)

Dies ist ein Lied	This is a song
Für dich allein:	For you alone,
Von kindischem Wähnen,	Of childish fears
Von frommen Tränen.	And fervent tears.
Durch Morgengärten klingt es	From dewy lawns it swings
Ein leichtbeschwingtes.	On weightless wings,
Nur dir allein	And only you
Möcht es ein Lied	This simple song
Das rühre sein.	Shall move to rue.

Stefan George

Translation by Olga Marx and Ernst Morwitz. Reprinted, by permission of the publisher, from *The Works of Stefan George Rendered Into English,* revised and enlarged edition, by Olga Marx and Ernst Morwitz. © 1974 The University of North Carolina Press.

b. Bagatelles for String Quartet, Opus 9, Nos. 4 and 5 (1913)

4

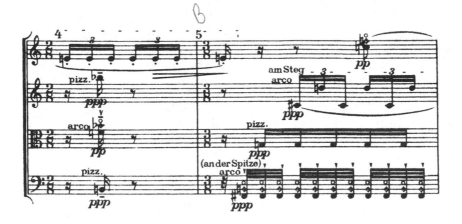

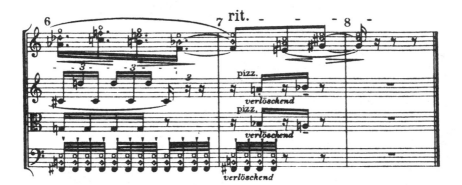

5

ANALYTICAL COMMENTS

Like the two pieces from Schoenberg's Op. 16, Webern's Op. 3 and Op. 9 represent distinct stages in the development of the composer's early atonal style. The Five Songs, Op. 3, written at the outset of the atonal period, still cling to relatively strict compositional techniques. The quasi-canonic procedures of mm. 6–7 are found throughout the piece, always employed with considerable freedom.[1] Thus mm. 1–3 of the voice are canonically (though not strictly) echoed by the top line of the piano in mm. 2–4. (In addition to differences in rhythm, G is inserted at m. 2.3, E at m. 4.1, and C at m. 4.2, and the last two notes of the voice in m. 3 are omitted.)

The overall form is a compact ternary, A (mm. 1–5)-B (6–7)-A' (8–12); the divisions are articulated by a ritard in m. 5 (in conjunction with a fragmentary repeat an octave lower of the piano's two highest pitches in m. 4, F^5–E^5) and by a low sustained chord with fermata at m. 7.4. The music is

---

1.   These procedures are discussed on pp. 79–80 of Morgan, *Twentieth-Century Music* (New York, 1990).

intimately tied to the text by Stefan George. The *A-B-A* structure follows the text's form and meaning; and the vocal line mirrors the rhyme scheme, *a-b-c-c-d-d-b-a-b,* with similar music for corresponding lines. Line seven is the exception, its music corresponding to that of lines three and four rather than two. This produces a rearrangement of content in the repeated *A* section, lending the voice part a more symmetrical structure:

As a further result, the voice now canonically follows the piano rather than precedes it, with the original relationship reestablished in the final three measures.

Symmetrical chords, common in much atonal music, play an important harmonic role. The opening piano chord, which also underlies the accompaniment in m. 2, is symmetrical (two major thirds separated by a perfect fifth). Other symmetrical chords appear at mm. 3.2, 4.1, and 10.2–12.2, the last elaborated melodically in both voice and piano. Perhaps prophetic of the later development of serialism, a retrograde of the first four pitches of the vocal line begins the *B* section: D-D♭-E♭-G♭ (mm. 2.2–3.1) become G♭-E♭-D♭-D (mm. 5.2–6.2).

The frequent appearance, in both melodic and harmonic form, of a pitch cell consisting of a major or minor third plus an internal half step—pitch sets (0,1,4) and (0,1,3) respectively—also lends intervallic consistency. Several melodic figures in mm. 1–4, for example, project the cell, and the opening chord contains both forms. Perhaps the most important interval is the falling minor second, the first melodic interval to appear, in both the voice and the top line of the piano (m. 1, D-D♭ in both cases). It occurs frequently throughout the song, often resulting from departures from strict canonic imitation (e.g., the piano's G-G♭ in m. 2.3).

The two Bagatelles, Op. 9, Nos. 4 and 5, illustrate the radically compressed, aphoristic instrumental style Webern explored during the years immediately preceding World War I. This style is characterized by extreme brevity, fragmentary textures, low dynamic levels (the strings play with mutes throughout both pieces), and special instrumental techniques. In the fourth Bagatelle it is nevertheless still possible to distinguish between melodic and accompanimental components, the former characterized by moving lines (second violin in mm. 1–3, counterpointed by viola and cello in mm. 1–2; first violin in mm. 5–8), the latter by immobile, ostinato-like repetitions (first violin in mm. 1–2 and 3–4; cello, viola, and second violin in mm. 5–8). Yet the melodic parts are also "athematic" to the extent that they contain no readily recognizable recurring motives.

Linear consistency is achieved, as in the Op. 3 song, through abstract, unordered pitch cells, the most important being a minor third plus minor second. Example 1 shows the derivation of the melodic parts of the first section from this cell. (All but one of these form pitch set 0,1,4, the exception—the second violin's B–G♯–A in m. 3—being the closely related(0,1,3). The only pitch not derived from the cell is the second violin's final D♯; but this, along with the preceding A, echoes the pitches of the first violin's opening ostinato figure (E♭–A).

EXAMPLE 1

Violin II, mm. 1–3   Cello, m. 2

The most important single interval is again the half step. Every note appears in close proximity to a note a minor second (or octave transposition) distant. Thus the second violin's opening B♭ sounds against the first violin's A and viola's B, while the first violin's E♭ is followed by the viola's E. This produces a related tendency to fill out chromatic scale segments: for example, eleven different pitches appear before B is repeated in m. 3.1, after which the missing G♯ is immediately sounded.

The Bagatelle is divisible into two equal parts, mm. 1–5.1 and 5–8, each consisting of a harmonic field established by the repeating accompanimental figures, plus a melodic overlay. The emphasis in the first half on the moving (melodic) parts shifts in the second to the more static "background." The melodic first violin in mm. 5–8, for example, contains two pitch repetitions (C and A♭), and it closes on A♭ (here spelled G♯), the repeated symmetrical center of the two three–note cells from which it is derived (Example 2):

EXAMPLE 2

Violin I, mm. 5–7

These repetitions, along with the now more static ostinatos, lend an added stability to the second section that, along with the ritard and decreasing rhythmic activity in mm. 7–8, provides a sort of cadence for the piece. (Repeating pitch patterns in conjunction with rhythmic dissolution offer a common means of achieving a sense of ending in atonal music.) The consistent use of different subdivisions of the measure produces complex rhythmic-textural relationships among the instruments. Indeed, much of the effect of the piece depends upon subtle manipulations of the rhythmic-textural surface.

The texture of the fifth Bagatelle is even more fragmentary and pointillistic; all distinction between melodic and accompanimental elements is dissolved. Although common intervallic content again provides a source of unity, here the analysis will focus on the larger linear motion, sketched in Example 3 in a simplified, de-rhythmicized form (all pitches are included, however). The music defines a wedge-shaped motion extending outward from the middle register of the opening. The half step is again critical, completely controlling the rising motion of the upper line to $A^{\flat 4}$ in m. 6. From this point the upward motion expands, first by a major second to $B^{\flat 4}$ (m. 7), then by a minor third to $C\sharp^5$ (m. 9) before concluding by rising a half step again to D^5 (m. 13).

The lower voice moves similarly, first downward chromatically to A^3 (m. 7), expanding immediately by a major second to G^3 and by a perfect fourth to D^3, but also concluding by half step, to $C\sharp^3$ (m. 13). Significantly, the final motion of this expanding structure, taking $C\sharp$ to D in the top voice and D to $C\sharp$ in the lower (the two parts exchanging pitches), is underlined instrumentally: the outer voices in m. 9 are played by the cello as a single melodic gesture from D^3 to $C\sharp^5$, while those in m. 13 are played by the viola, from $C\sharp^3$ to D^5.

EXAMPLE 3

12

WEBERN
String Quartet, Opus 28 (1929), second movement

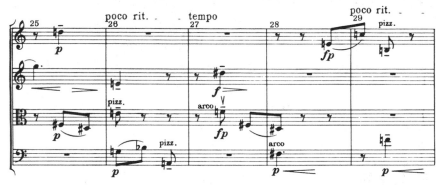

ANALYTICAL COMMENTS

The middle movement of the String Quartet, Op. 28, a three-part "Scherzo," illustrates the general stylistic traits of Webern's mature twelve-tone music—extreme brevity, wide intervals, transparent texture, and relatively simple surface rhythm—and his tendency to exploit structural features of the row in making compositional choices. The first twelve pitches of the first violin part project the prime form (P-0) of the row, made up of three closely related tetrachords:

EXAMPLE 1

Each tetrachord presents a particular ordering of a four-note chromatic scale segment. Since the three chromatic segments, whose lowest pitches are respectively B, G, and D♯, divide the octave into equal major thirds, the two transpositions of the prime by major third—P-4 and P-8—preserve the unordered tetrachordal structure of the original, as do R-0, R-4, and R-8. These six forms, the only ones with this property, are used exclusively in the movement.

The three tetrachords are also related by serial operations: the third tetrachord of P-0 is a transposition of the first a major third higher, the second is its retrograde a major third lower. This feature determines the row successions in the first main section (mm. 1–18), the last tetrachord of each row becoming simultaneously the first tetrachord of the following one. Rows are presented linearly in each instrument, producing the succession P-0—P-4—P-8, for example, in mm. 1–17 of the first violin part. Since each of these transpositions takes the row up a major third, the third (P-8) returns to P-0 (i.e., pitches 9–12 of P-8 equal pitches 1–4 of P-0), bringing about an exact repetition of the entire first section. At the end of the repeat there is no overlap, so that the final row closes off the section.

This overlapping principle is maintained in all instruments throughout the first section, a four-voiced canon with two *P*-form voices and two *R*-form voices, distributed as shown in Table 1.

TABLE 1

vn I	*P*-0 / *P*-4 / *P*-8 / *P*-0 / *P*-4 / *P*-8
vn II	*R*-4 / *R*-0 / *R*-8 / *R*-4 / *R*-0 / *R*-8
va	*P*-4 / *P*-8 / *P*-0 / *P*-4 / *P*-8 / *P*-0
vc	*R*-0 / *R*-8 / *R*-4 / *R*-0 / *R*-8 / *R*-4

(Since in this row *R*-forms are identical to *I*-forms, the canon is actually both by retrograde and by inversion.)

The four voices are in rhythmic canon as well, with a quarter-note delay between entries (in the order vn I-vc-vn II-va). The rhythmic sequence, consisting entirely of quarter notes (including both attacks and rests), is established by violin I and strictly followed by the viola. In the retrograde voices (vn II, vc) the canonic structure is broken by the omission of certain pitches, each omitted note being replaced by a rest. The F that "should" appear in the cello in m. 3.2 (fourth pitch of *R*-0) is replaced by a rest, as are pitches at mm. 6.2 and 13.2 in the cello and at mm. 4.1, 7.1, 11.2, and 13.1 in violin II. In all cases, the missing note appears in another voice, on either the preceding beat or the same one. Although violin II and the cello thus have a somewhat different rhythmic structure, they too form a rhythmic canon with each other throughout most of the section. Contrary to traditional canonic practice, melodic contour is varied throughout, lending variety to an extremely restricted underlying structure.

The second section (mm. 19–36) is set off by a faster tempo, consistently arco bowing, more differentiated rhythm, and a more fragmentary texture. The distribution of rows is also new, although the same forms are used as before, as seen in Table 2.

TABLE 2

mm. 19–27	mm. 27–36
R-4 vn I (pitches 1–6)	→ va (7–9); vc (10–12)
P-8 vn II (1–6)	→ vc (7–9); vn II (10–12)
P-0 va (1–12)	*P*-4 va (1–3); vn I (4–6 / 7–9); vn II (10–11); vn I (12)
R-8 vc (1–12)	*R*-0 vn II (1–3); vn I (4–6); va (7–9); vn I (10–12)

(Since in this section certain rows are presented by more than one player, this table is organized by row form rather than instrument.) The two subsections, mm. 19–27 and 27–36, are defined by complete row presentations: *P*-0 and *R*-8 in the first (va and vc, respectively) and *P*-4 and *R*-0 in the second (alternating vn I, vn II, and va). Two additional rows, *R*-4 and *P*-8, span the entire section, six notes appearing in each half (vn I and vn II respectively, in the first half, alternating instruments in the second). The halves of R-4 are separated by an extended pause (mm. 26–29).

The rhythmic structure of the new section is also more complex than that of the first. R-4 and P-8 are in strict rhythmic canon (the repeated F♯ in the cello at m. 36.1 is the only exception), at a distance of six eighth notes between the voices throughout and with a switch of leading voice from R-4 to P-8 after the first half (beginning in the cello, m. 28). Here the canon is brought out by a strict inversional contour between the two voices. Different durations are introduced into the basic rhythmic structure, although the interval between successive attacks is always four eighth notes.

The two other canonic voices, first R-8 and P-0 and then P-4 and R-0, feature groups of three eighth notes. These rows are also in strict rhythmic canon during the first half of the section, with each three-note unit in strict contour inversion with the corresponding unit from the other row; but in the second half their rhythmic relationship varies, perhaps to create "structural tension" before the recapitulation. The only exception to the three-note instrumental division of this row pair occurs on the final note of the middle section, where the A♭ of P-4 overlaps with the first pitch of the final section and is thus played by violin I, pizzicato (m. 36.5), instead of violin II. (Pizzicatos have been gradually introduced since m. 26, however, mediating between the two sections.)

The final section (mm. 37–53) is in essence a repeat of the first, using the same set of overlapping rows but rotating them in relation to the instrumental layout:

TABLE 3

	1st row, 1st section	1st row, 3rd section
vn I	P-0	R-4
vn II	R-4	P-4
va	P-4	R-0
vc	R-0	P-0

Although the order of entrances is altered, as is the pattern of "borrowed" notes and corresponding rests, the underlying framework of rhythms and pitches remains as before, except that the final tetrachords of the second ending are played at a faster tempo, providing a brief, accelerated coda.

Webern once remarked that this movement could be thought of either as a Scherzo and Trio or as an A-B-A song form with a developmental middle section. Although the easily perceptible contrasting features of the middle section support the former interpretation, the middle section also develops the canonic idea of the outer ones. In this connection, two points regarding the return of material from the first section in the last are interesting: unlike a normal Scherzo, the return is considerably varied; and it retains the repeat, so that the cyclical nature of the row successions can again be exploited.

13

EDGARD VARÈSE (1883–1965)

Hyperprism (1923)

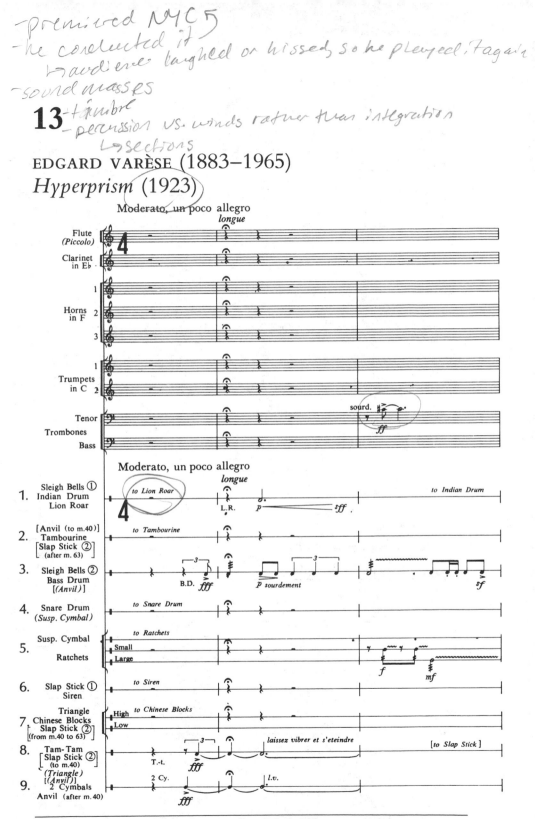

Reprinted by kind permission of G. Ricordi & C. SpA, Milano, copyright owners.

*) ⟩ = frapper avec la main
≢ = agiter et secouer

**) R = sur le rebord (Rim)
M = membrane (Head)

rhythmic independence b/t top & bottom

*) Frotter rudement membrane avec le pouce

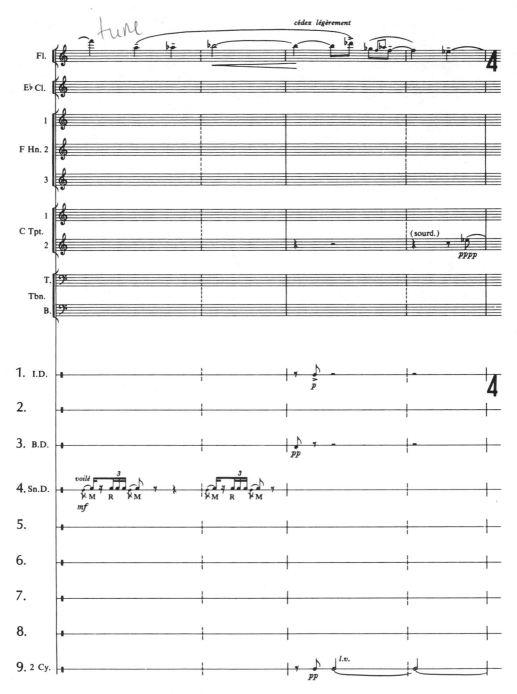

—not serial, but intervalic & how the intervals are placed.

*) dans le ⟨—⟩ comme le ⟨—⟩ la 1ère Trompette legèrement dominante

Varèse's music — dramatic*

ABCDC

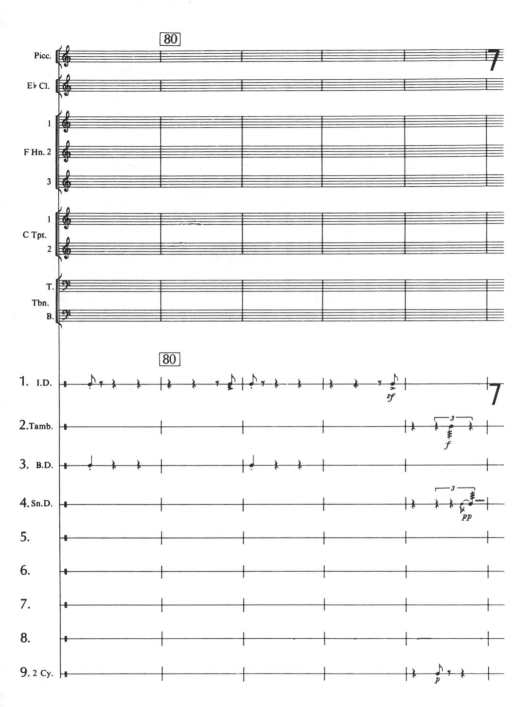

SUGGESTED POSITION OF PERCUSSION PLAYERS AND INSTRUMENTS:

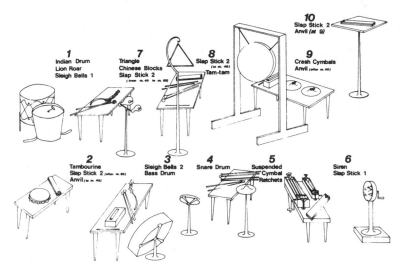

PLAYER 1
INDIAN DRUM
should be played with the
hand or with a pair of very
soft FELT BEATERS
LION ROAR
SLEIGH BELLS 1
on a handle

PLAYER 2
TAMBOURINE
in the absence of a tenth
player:

[**SLAP STICK 2**
(to be obtained from
Player 7 at m. 63)
ANVIL consisting of a
metal tube about 9" long
and 1 3/4" thick laying
free on a wood block in
an indentation lined with
felt; to be hit with a
METAL ROD about
1/8" thick and 6" long;
to m. 40)]

PLAYER 3
SLEIGH BELLS 2
on a handle
BASS DRUM
as large and deep as possible

PLAYER 4
SNARE DRUM
should be 6-7" deep;
played normally
on membrane except when
otherwise indicated
(M - membrane; R- rim;
snares off)

PLAYER 5
SUSPENDED CYMBAL
(Cymbals Chinoise) very
large
2 RACHETS (small and
large) cranked

PLAYER 6
SLAP STICK 1
SIREN low, with brake
mechanism

PLAYER 7
2 CHINESE BLOCKS
(high and low)
TRIANGLE
in the absence of a tenth
player:
[**SLAP STICK 2**
(from m. 40 to m. 63)]

PLAYER 8
TAM-TAM or GONG
very deep and rich;
in the absence of a tenth
player:
[**SLAP STICK 2**
(to m. 40)]

PLAYER 9
2 CRASH CYMBALS
in the absence of a tenth
player:
[**ANVIL**
(after m. 40)]

(PLAYER 10)
SLAP STICK 2
ANVIL

ANALYTICAL COMMENTS

Despite its brevity, *Hyperprism* is a fully realized example of the innovative music Varèse developed during the 1920s. The work's originality is evident even in the choice of instruments: two woodwinds (with flute doubling piccolo), seven brass, and a percussion section that includes sixteen different instruments, among them such curiosities as lion's roar and siren. The extreme registral range extends from bass trombone to piccolo, and the percussion group includes high, medium, and low instruments from each nonpitched family (skins, metals, and woods).

Varèse rarely blends these instruments but rather emphasizes their differences, in separate musical planes defined by timbre, register, and density, typically combined into composite, multilayered textures. Musical coherence is not derived primarily from such traditional procedures as thematic-motivic development and linear progression but from the development of these textural entities.

There are three main sections, set off by significant contrasts: mm. 1–29, 30–58, and 59–81. The first is basically moderato (with a number of internal tempo changes) and has highly varied and polyphonically differentiated wind textures, combined with elaborate percussion writing that is largely independent of the pitched instruments. The second section, at a slower tempo, opens with a more homophonically conceived texture; the percussion group, playing an essentially supportive role, is in general less active than before. The third section returns to the moderato tempo of the first and brings back material from both previous sections.

The opening trombone gesture, based on repetitions of a single note, conforms to a type much favored by Varèse. It holds $C\sharp^4$ for eleven measures, subjecting it to transformations through different patterns of repetition, changing dynamic levels, and timbral development. The changes in timbre result from the transference of the pitch from trombone to horn, which occurs four times (mm. 3.4, 5, 7, 8.3), dividing the passage into several subunits. In addition, the $C\sharp$ is decorated from its second appearance by chromatic grace-note extensions, first below and then above, eventually encompassing a major third on both sides of the original pitch. The last of these decorations (m. 11), in the first horn rather than trombone as before, leads to a transference of the $C\sharp^4$ up an octave in m. 12.

The unusually static nature of the pitch structure in these measures reflects Varèse's tendency to view musical progression and development in textural and "spatial" rather than linear terms. Thus the opening $C\sharp$ seems to have little inclination to move linearly, but the idea of symmetrical expansion outward suggested by its grace-note decorations in mm. 1–11 proves critical for the piece's organization. The D^2 introduced in m. 4.4 (bass trombone) and the answering C^6 in m. 12 (flute), the first added pitches other than the grace notes, are symmetrically positioned around $C\sharp^4$.

The initial outward expansions lead to a tutti chord in mm. 15–16, the first of several climactic moments that punctuate the piece. Typically, the chord is not attacked and released as a unit but gradually assembled from separate components (mm. 12–15), then filtered out until only the highest note (C^6) remains (m. 18), overlapping with the beginning of the next subsection. Notable among this chord's components (the next to last to be removed) is the octave-transferred C$\sharp$ of the opening gesture, which has persisted throughout the entire segment.

The new subsection opens with a radical reduction in forces (mm. 19ff.), then builds quickly to two sustained sonorities (mm. 23–25, 27–29) that are combined with the richest percussion texture yet. The second of these sonorities includes the highest pitch in the first main section, A^6 (piccolo); this pitch together with a simultaneous $B\flat^5$ (clarinet) forms a major seventh that, measured in reference to the opening C$\sharp^4$, is symmetrically positioned with the major seventh associated with the section's lowest pitch, F^1-E^2 in m. 15 (trombones).[1]

A fermata closes the first section at this climactic point (m. 29), and the second section opens immediately thereafter. Despite the high degree of contrast between the two sections, common elements remain. The repeated-note idea is retained at m. 30, given a new form and character, as is the general idea of expanding outward from a relatively low opening. Indeed, the gradual accumulation of the sustained climactic chord in mm. 40–43 corresponds roughly to that of mm. 14–16 (though here the expansion is exclusively upward), and this chord, like the previous one, is followed by further upward expansions, reaching full extent at mm. 46–47 (corresponding to mm. 27–29). Here, however, the spatial extent is retained until the end of the section (m. 58, with mm. 48–54 acting as an interruption). Moreover, the texture of the passages beginning at mm. 43–47 and 55–58, in many respects the most complex in the composition, can be viewed as a highly differentiated application of the repeated-note idea. The underlying sonority is separated into its constituent parts and reassembled, each strand undergoing a different pattern of repetition.

Like the first section, the last begins (m. 59) in a relatively low register with a repeated-note figure in the brass decorated by both upper and lower grace-note extensions (the repeated pitch is now F$\sharp^3$ rather than C$\sharp^4$, and played by horn rather than trombone). The opening idea is compressed: there is only one timbral transference, reversed (from horn to trombone), and the release of the repeated F$\sharp$ into a melodic configuration occurs more quickly, at mm. 65–67 (balancing the flute's melodic release, following its sustained C^6, in mm. 19–22).

The subsequent upper-register expansion also recurs (beginning at m. 68), but is now realized through material derived from the second section (rather than mm. 23–29 from the first). The piccolo and clarinet bring back the register and general interval structure of their figures from mm. 46–58;

---

1.   For a more detailed consideration of symmetrical relationships in *Hyperprism* see Jonathan W. Bernard, *The Music of Edgard Varèse* (New Haven, 1987), pp. 193–217.

and the horns later (m. 84) take up a figure closely related in rhythm, texture, and timbre to their material from mm. 30–38 (especially the last one and a half measures). This horn figure now provides a final climactic surge, leading to the formation of the last tutti chord, which contains the highest note in *Hyperprism,* the piccolo's G^7 (anticipated in m. 72). This chord is the only tutti whose appearance coincides with the close of a major section; the tuttis of the previous two sections (mm. 16 and 43) articulate only internal subdivisions (their less conclusive function is underscored by the retention of pitches into the next section: the flute and clarinet's C-C♯ in mm. 16–17, the first horn's B in mm. 43–44).

Although in the outer sections the percussion parts are largely independent of the pitched instruments, they do share certain rhythmic ideas with the winds. The many repeated-note wind figures produce especially strong associations with the percussion, where repeated figures tend to be the norm. Percussion motives also help define the work's larger formal shape. The loud, sustained cymbal figure that opens the piece, for example, brought back in various forms within the first section (mm. 5, 7, 12, 16), reappears several times at the beginning of the third section (mm. 60, 62, 64, 66). The eighth-note figure in the Indian drum at m. 6 (also in the sleigh bells, m. 24) and the snare-drum figure in m. 10 (also mm. 21, 25) both reappear in m. 61, just as the third section is getting under way.

This discussion has focused primarily on the movement's overall design rather than on details of pitch structure. For the latter, it must suffice to mention—in addition to the tendency toward symmetrical distributions— that Varèse, like other nontonal composers, relies upon recurring interval configurations to achieve pitch consistency. *Hyperprism* also reveals a tendency to complete chromatic aggregates (all twelve pitches of the tempered scale, regardless of order) within formal units. Thus in the first unit (mm. 1–16), the opening C♯ is absorbed into a chromatic segment encompassing eight half steps, from B♭ up through F♯, the aggregate being completed with the appearance of the tutti chord in m. 15.

14

ALBAN BERG (1885–1935)

Five Orchestral Songs, Opus 4 (*Altenberg Lieder*) (1912)

    a. No. 2, *Sahst du nach dem Gewitterregen den Wald?*

Sahst du nach dem Gewitterregen den Wald?!?!
Alles rastet, blinkt und ist schöner als zuvor,
Siehe, Fraue, auch du brauchst Gewitterregen!

Peter Altenberg

After the summer rain did you see the forest?!?!
All is glitter, quiet, and more beautiful than before,
See, good woman, you too sometimes need summer rainstorms!

b. No. 5, *Hier ist Friede*

Hier ist Friede. Hier weine ich mich aus
über alles!
Hier löst sich mein unfaßtbares, un-
ermeßliches Leid, das mir die
Seele verbrennt.

Here is peace, here my tears flow, my
head weeps out its sadness!
Here I give cry to my unfathomable,
measureless sorrow that would
consume my very soul.

Siehe, hier sind keine Menschen, keine
 Ansiedlungen.
Hier ist Friede! Hier tropft Schnee leise
 in Wasserlachen.

Behold, not a sign of mankind, not a
 soul around me.
Here is peace! Here the snow drops
 softly into pools of water.

Peter Altenberg

ANALYTICAL COMMENTS

Alban Berg's *Altenberg Lieder,* five orchestral songs composed several years after his formal studies with Schoenberg and after he had abandoned traditional tonality, are settings of texts by Peter Altenberg, a well-known Viennese contemporary of the composer who specialized in aphoristic poems written on picture postcards.[1] While the extreme brevity of the songs, notably the three middle ones, recalls works by Schoenberg and (especially) Webern, the sustained melodic character of Berg's music, with its relatively clear motivic and thematic correspondences, remains closely tied to nineteenth-century practice, as does its harmonic language, which emphasizes mildly dissonant combinations commonly found in chromatic tonal music. (At one point—m. 35 of the fifth song—there is even an unadorned A-major triad.)

Even in the second song, where the brevity and textural contrast reflect the aphoristic, fragmentary quality of Altenberg's text, the voice provides an element of linear continuity that spans the piece. It contains two important recurrences of the four-note falling motive first heard in m. 2 (E♭-B♭-A-E): at the voice's climax in m. 8 (transposed upward by a tritone and with the fourth note altered, though the expected B♭ appears as the next voice pitch) and again at the original pitch level in the voice's last four pitches in m. 10.

 In addition, the entire voice part from m. 8 on, including both of these recurrences, is canonically imitated by the cello. The untransposed falling figure of m. 2 thus appears as the last melodic event of the song, its final E♮ resolving upward to the final F octave in the double bass in m. 11, almost like a leading tone. An octave F is also the first note to appear in the accompaniment (m. 2, where it also "resolves" the voice's previous E), and forms the bass of the climactic chord at m. 7, providing a veiled yet significant tonal anchor that links opening, climax, and closing.

 The recurring melodic figure from m. 2 contains two perfect fourths con-

1. For an analytical view of the entire opus, see Mark De Voto, "Some Notes on the Unknown *Altenberg Lieder," Perspectives of New Music,* 5, no. 1 (1966): 37–74.

nected by a half step (pitch set 0,1,4,5). This same intervallic combination appears, reordered and transposed, as the last four voice notes in m. 4 (E♭–A♭–A–D); fourths also figure prominently in the accompanimental upbeat figures in the cello (m. 6) and celesta (mm. 8–9). However, most of the orchestra part is derived from a three-note cell consisting of a major third encompassing a minor second (set 0,1,4). Berg employs this cell too, not so much as an abstract interval configuration but melodically, with readily audible motivic parallelisms. Notice especially the extended series of rising thirds that results from the concatenation of the cell in the opening phrase of the orchestra part: E–G♯ (viola, m. 3), B–D♯ and D–F♯ (horn, mm. 3–4), A–C♯ and C–E (clarinet, m. 4), F–A, A♭–C, and G–B (bassoon, mm. 4–5), culminating in the trumpet's rising B–D♯–F♯ in m. 6, which introduces the climactic chord at m. 7. The lower third of this last figure, B–D♯, is heard twice, in the flute (m. 5) and trombone (m. 6), before the trumpet carries it on to F♯; the repetitions add intensity as the climax approaches.

The fifth song, one of the most remarkable creations of the Viennese atonal period, is even more tightly structured. Most of its content is derived from four basic thematic ideas that recur repeatedly, usually at the same pitch level and with only minor (if any) modifications:

EXAMPLE 1

A. Cello, mm. 1–5

B. Flute, mm. 5–9   (12-tone theme)

C. Bassoon, mm. 8–12

D. Oboe, mm. 10–13

D′. Trombone, mm. 13–15

D″. Violin, mm. 14–15

Table 1 lists the most important recurrences of these themes, grouped (approximately) by sectional division:

TABLE 1

Section	Measures	Thematic content
1	1–5	A (bass cl and vc, mm. 1–5)
2	5–10	B (fl and harp, mm. 5–10); C (bn, 4th trbn, and b, mm. 7–12)
3	10–15	A (3rd hn, doubled by accented notes in vc, mm. 11–15); B (1st hn and va, mm. 10–15); D (ob, mm. 11–13); D' (3rd trbn, mm. 13–15); D'' (1st vn and tpt, mm. 14–15)
4	15–20	A elaborated (harp, mm. 18–19); B transposed (b to vc to b, mm. 15–20)
5	20–25	A elaborated (ctrbn, ctrtuba, harp, and pf, mm. 20–25); A transposed and in diminution (str and ww figuration, mm. 20–25); B incomplete (v, mm. 19–23)
6	25–30	C (harp, 4th trbn, and bass cl, mm. 25–26); A elaborated (v, mm. 25–29); B incomplete (solo va, mm. 27–29); C (solo vn, mm. 26–27)
7	30–35	A elaborated (upper ww, hn, 3rd and 4th trbn, xyl, va, and vc, mm. 30–35); B (vn, mm. 29–34); C (bass cl, bn, ctrtuba, tpt, 1st and 2nd trbn, and b, mm. 31–35)
8	35–40	A as chord (harp, m. 36); D and derivatives, imitated (v and 1st vn, mm. 36–39; hn, mm. 36–38; vc, mm. 37–38; va and trbn, mm. 38–40)
9	40–45	B extended (bn, v, and pf, mm. 39–46); C (bass cl and harp, mm. 42–46)
10	45–50	A elaborated (hn and solo vc, mm. 46–50)
11	50–55	A (solo str, doubled by final notes of lines in trbn and 1st tpt, plus 2nd vn pizz, mm. 54–55); A as chord (ww, pf, and harp, mm. 54–55)

The principal melodic ideas reveal a number of common features, especially shared opening and closing pitches. Thus E♮ is the last pitch of both theme A and theme B, and the first pitch of theme C; while C♮ is the first pitch of theme B and the last pitch of theme C. The E that closes theme B is often followed by an upper neighbor F, duplicating the first two pitches of D in reverse order (brought out in mm. 9–11, for example, when the flute's E^4-F^4 is immediately echoed by the oboe's F^5-E^5). Berg exploits these pitch connections to join the themes in a virtually seamless web. The constant appearance of the same pitches (C, E, and F—plus G as the first note of theme *A*) at points of formal division and elision also produces an elusive "tonal" flavor that, despite the prevailing atonality, preserves the notion that some pitches have more structural weight than others. The bass G that sounds through most of the next-to-last section (mm. 45–49, repeated) and through the entire last one (mm. 51–54, sustained), and that supplies the bass of the final chordal statements of theme *A* (mm. 54–55) is an especially stabilizing influence at the close.

The formal structure outlined in Table 1, with its eleven sections of equal length, is articulated primarily by recurrences of the four essentially fixed melodic elements, lending the song something of the quality of a passacaglia (as Berg notes in his tempo indication). This is not a normal passacaglia, however; there are several recurring themes of roughly equal importance rather than just one, and none of these appears in every section (although *A*, either as a melody or chord, occurs in all but two). And in a typical passacaglia the individual sections form a series of clearly segmented variations, whereas the sections in this song overlap with one another and are themselves overlapped by the recurring themes, merging into an unbroken continuum. The quality of ongoing development—building to climactic points at m. 25 and (more intensely) m. 35—helps explain why, despite all its technical novelty, this song so clearly belongs within the domain of late musical Romanticism.

15

BERG
Lyric Suite (1926), first movement

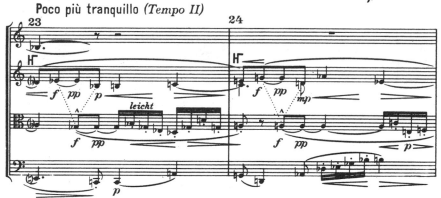

Poco più tranquillo *(Tempo II)*

accel.

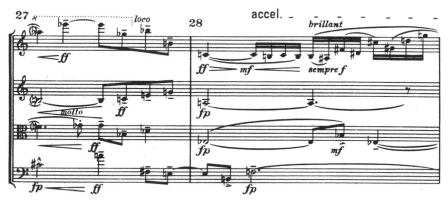

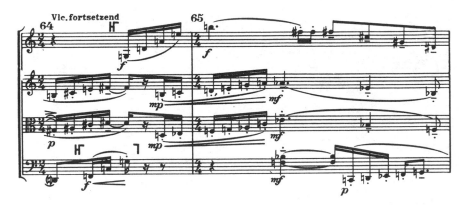

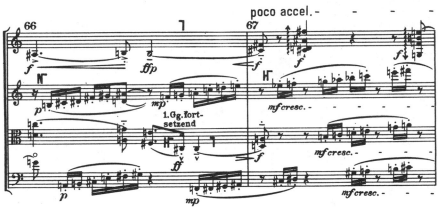

ANALYTICAL COMMENTS

Let us first look at some of the properties of the twelve-tone row of this movement (Example la).[1] The unordered content of each hexachord forms a six-note diatonic segment that can be represented either as a scale or as a series of perfect fifths. Berg exploits both possibilities, reordering the hexachords to form two secondary rows (Examples 1b and 1c). Moreover, the perfect-fifth series is "hidden" within the original row, appearing as every other note in each hexachord in the sequence 1-3-5-6-4-2 / 12-10-8-7-9-11 (Example 1d).

Berg brings out the fifths in the first thematic presentation of the row (vn I, mm. 2–4) through articulation and contour (the regular down-up alterations), preparing the introduction of the row in fifths in the cello, mm. 7.2–9.1. The scalar version is also prepared, in this case not through the internal structure of the row itself but through Berg's preference for diatonic stepwise motion in determining the surface distribution of the row. (The viola line in mm. 3–4 and all three upper lines in m. 5, for instance, move consistently by step, yet none is derived from the original row.)

EXAMPLE 1

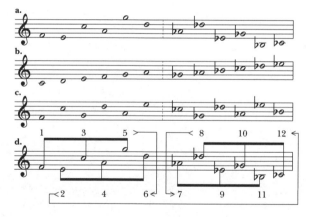

Another significant feature is that the row begins on F and ends on B, a tritone apart; therefore all row forms that begin with one of these pitches end with the other. This enables Berg to use a closed system of eight rows, bounded by these two pitches: *P*-0, *R*-0, *I*-0, *RI*-0, *P*-6, *R*-6, *I*-6, *RI*-6.[2] Moreover, since the second half of the row is a retrograde of the first half, transposed at the tritone, each *R* form is identical to the *P* form beginning at a tritone distance, as is each *RI* form to the tritone-related *I* form. The

---

1.   For additional comments, see Morgan, *Twentieth-Century Music* (New York, 1991), pp. 214–16.
2.   This resembles the eight-row system used in Schoenberg's Suite, op. 25, discussed ibid., pp. 189–90.

EXAMPLE 2

eight rows are thus reduced to four, here designated as *P-0*, *P-6*, *I-0*, and *I-6* (Example 2). Berg confines himself largely to these four throughout this movement. The following table reveals the close correspondences between changes of row groupings and formal divisions in the movement.

TABLE 1

| Section | | Part I | | | Part II | |
	mm.	row forms		mm.	row forms
I	1–12	P-0 / I-6		33.2–39	P-0 / I-6
				40–42.1	P-3 / I-9
				42.1–48	P-0 / I-6
II	13–15.1	P-0 / I-6 / P-6 / I-0		48–51.1	P-0 / I-6 / P-6
III	15.2–17	P-0 / P-3/P-6 / P-9		51.2–53.1	P-6 / I-0 / I-3 / I-9
	18–23	I-0 / I-3 / I-6 / I-9			
IV	22.3–33	P-0 / I-6 / P-6 / I-0 / P-9		53.1–69	P-0 / I-6 / P-6 / I-3 / P-9

The only rows Berg uses outside the basic group of four are *P-3*, *I-9*, *P-9*, and *I-3*, which collectively form a transposition of the original group a minor third higher. This new group is of course also tritone-related, framed by D and A♭. Together the four framing pitches of the two groups divide the octave symmetrically by minor thirds: F–A♭–B–D. Berg emphasizes this division by employing the second group only in conjunction with the first, joining two rows from each group to form a four-row group defined by the complete minor-third cycle. (The only exception is the single *P-9* row in the cello at mm. 26.4–33.1.) In m. 15, for example, when rows from the second group appear for the first time, *P-0* and *P-6* (first group) are combined with *P-9* and *P-3* (second group), beginning respectively on F, B, D, and A♭. Berg stresses the minor-third relation by assigning each row to a different instrument, starting all four simultaneously to produce a relatively sustained "diminished-seventh" chord.

As in other Berg works, the detailed distribution of row forms is often ambiguous, follows no consistent pattern, and contains occasional alterations in order. Typical are mm. 1–9, whose row content is analyzed in Example 3. (Arrows indicate row transfers from one instrument to another, and two arrows mean the row splits into two directions; repeated notes are placed in parentheses.) Except for the row in fifths, presented chordally in m. 1 and linearly from m. 7.2 (cello), only P-0 and I-6 are used. A complete statement of P-0 appears in the first violin in mm. 2–4.1, but all other statements of both P-0 and I-6 are distributed among several instruments. Extended row segments appear melodically in the cello (pitches 2–8 of I-6, mm. 4.3–5) and second violin (pitches 5–8 of P-0, m. 6), but, significantly, these usually do not represent the main line (marked H). Even the three-note first-violin figure in m. 5 and its literal repetition an octave lower (cello, m. 6) are drawn from different rows.

Only in m. 7, when the first violin presents a varied restatement of the main thematic idea, once more derived from P-0, does an extended row segment again assume thematic import. But although the rhythm and general contour of this return mirror the original almost exactly (the down–up alternations are absent), the row is rotated relative to the theme, beginning on the ninth pitch and ending on the eighth. The unison and octave imitations in the viola, violin II, and violin I in the next two measures typify Berg's twelve-tone writing; the overlapping statements of the same configurations produce an almost harmonic effect (fully realized in mm. 10–11 when pitches 4–6 of P-0 are "frozen" to initiate the cadential gesture concluding in m. 12). A similar effect is found in m. 4, when the first note of I-6 (violin I) splits into two continuations, the first heard in the first half of the measure, the second in the second half.

Another factor influencing row distribution is a tendency to employ triadic harmonic configurations. Triadic successions in the row itself offer some opportunities—for example, the Gb-major and A-minor triads in the upper three parts at mm. 5.1 and 5.3, derived from pitches 9–11 of I-6 and 2–4 of P-0. But such other triad-based harmonies as the dominant-seventh and diminished-seventh chords in m. 7 (first quarter and last eighth) are drawn from two different rows. The harmony of mm. 15ff., strongly influenced by the diminished-seventh-chord relationship of the four rows (see above), also has triadic suggestions.

As indicated in Table 1, the formal divisions of the movement, often described as a sonata form without development, are closely tied to the row structure. The first section of Part I opens with the basic pair P-0 / I-6, the second adds their tritone transpositions P-6 / I-0 to complete the basic four-row group, and the third, partly transitional in nature, uses two successive minor-third groups (creating a sort of "modulation"). The fourth and final section (the "second theme," with a new tempo and contrasting melodic, rhythmic, and textural character) brings back the original group, plus a P-9 held over from the third section.

EXAMPLE 3

row in fifths (cello)

Part II restates this structure with significant departures: (1) two rows from the second group are inserted in the first section (mm. 40–42); (2) a different minor-third group appears in the "transition" (mm. 51–53); (3) *I*-3 is substituted for *I*-0 in the fourth section (and *P*-9 is now only suggested). The analogy between row relationships and tonal relationships, though certainly suggestive, is thus not exact.

The relationships of the musical events in Part II to those in Part I prove to be even more complex:

TABLE 2

Section	Part I	Part II
	m. 1	—
I	mm. 2–6	mm. 35.3–39
	—	mm. 40–41
	mm. 7–12	mm. 42–48
II	mm. 13–15.1	mm. 49–51.1
III	mm. 15.2–17	mm. 51.2–53.1
	mm. 18–22	—
IV	mm. 23–32	mm. 53–61
	mm. 33–35	mm. 62–68
	—	m. 69

The first section of Part II is lengthened (though m. 1 is missing, mm. 40–41 are added), and the third is shortened (mm. 18–22 are omitted). And though the content of the two halves is close enough to trace measure-by-measure correspondences, Part II significantly varies the material throughout, relying largely upon rhythm, texture, and contour for establishing connections.

To some extent the first section (mm. 2–12) sets the pattern for the movement's overall shape: an initial thematic statement (mm. 2–4) leads to a more relaxed, cadential passage (mm. 5–6), followed by a more climactic return of the thematic material (mm. 7–11) and a second cadential passage (m. 12). The movement as a whole is punctuated by a series of such climactic returns of the opening material, producing a dynamic shape only partially consistent with the sonata idea. Thus in mm. 20–23, the end of the "transition," the opening theme returns at the original pitch level, in a more elaborate textural environment and with the first hexachord an octave higher. And the final segment of the more relaxed second group (mm. 33–35), rather than being a "closing group," forms an extended "upbeat," an accelerating buildup (including the first sixteenth-note scalar rows) to the return of the opening thematic idea that begins Part II (m. 36).

This opening idea thus enters as a climactic culmination rather than simply a restatement. Moreover, only its second half seems to be present, although the missing rising sixteenth-note portion of the theme (as in m. 2) is rhythmically represented by the violins in m. 35 (in practice indistinguishable from the other rising six-note scales). Indeed, the entire theme here proves to be derived from the scalar row (which thus continues from the previous section) rather than from *P*-0, so that its recognizability depends entirely upon rhythm and contour.

Like mm. 2–12, mm. 36–48 form a two-phased development consisting of the first thematic statement (mm. 36–37) and cadential gesture (mm. 38–39), plus a second, more climactic thematic statement and cadence. This climactic restatement is much more intense: not only are the quasi-canonic returns (mm. 44.3–47) registrally higher than at mm. 7–11, but the leading voice here has a complete statement of the theme (mm. 42–44.1), literal and at the original pitch level, and played *forte,* split between the viola and cello (so that the "hidden" fifths are projected instrumentally). In addition, two new measures (mm. 40–41) provide an upbeat to this return, building toward it with faster rhythmic motion, rising contour, a crescendo, and an accelerando.

This new return, along with its imitative development (mm. 42–47), represents the movement's principal climax; its importance is underscored by the omission of mm. 18–22, encompassing the thematic return from the end of the transition and its upbeat. In compensation, an additional thematic statement is inserted at mm. 64–66 that provides a closing counterweight to the main climax. It also makes up for the fact that mm. 65–68 can no longer build up to a statement of the main theme (as did mm. 32–35), but now lead to the final cadence. The simplified contour of this final thematic statement suggests that the end is near. Derived from the perfect-fifth row, it also balances the scalar version of the theme at mm. 35–37.1. The final cadence itself (m. 69), without counterpart at the end of the first half, balances the introductory measure.

-in the U.S. teaching in Yale
-Triadic
-Not traditional harmony, but tonal
-Pastoral character
-Rounded binary

16

PAUL HINDEMITH (1895–1963)

Ludus tonalis (1942), second *Interludium* and third *Fuga*

Form defined by unusual means
Pastorale, moderate (♩. ca 50)
Interludium
p
5
pp
mp
chromatic linear progression
B
10
p
mf
piu f
15
f
pp
20
mp
rit.
p
G cadence

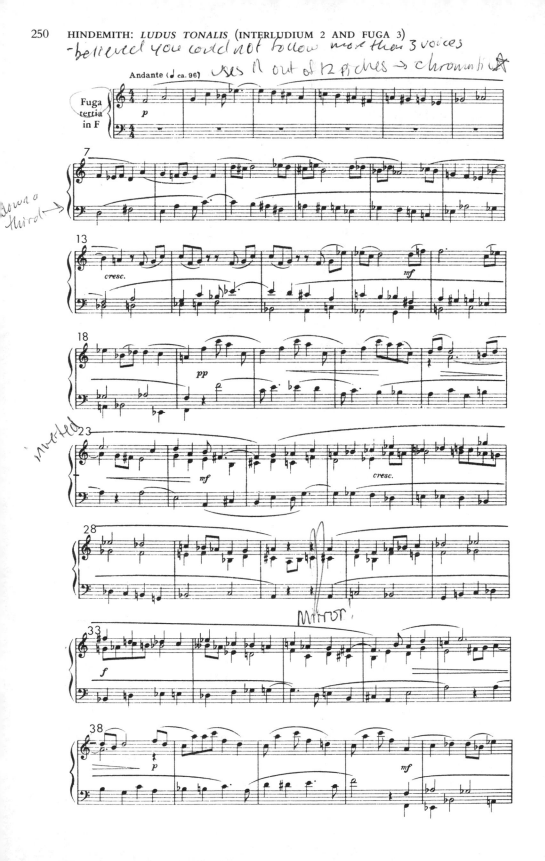

ANALYTICAL COMMENTS

Hindemith's *Ludus tonalis (Play of Tones)* is a collection of twenty-five piano pieces, containing a prelude, twelve fugues, eleven interludes separating the fugues, and a postlude. The fact that tonal centers of the fugues represent all twelve chromatic pitches recalls Bach's *Well-Tempered Clavier,* while the prevalence of "learned" contrapuntal devices (e.g., the postlude is a strict retrograde inversion of the prelude) evokes Bach's *Art of Fugue.* Like those compositions, *Ludus tonalis* is didactic in nature (it is subtitled "Studies in Counterpoint, Tonal Organization, and Piano Playing"), conceived as a practical demonstration of the new compositional philosophy Hindemith adopted during the early 1930s.

Form, tonality, thematic order, texture, and "pastoral" character combine in the second *Interludium* to present a clearly organized structure with markedly traditional features. The form is binary; the music begins and ends securely on G, and the principal division is articulated by a cadence on D, the dominant (m. 10). Despite suggestions of triadic sonorities (e.g., the left hand in mm. 1–4), the harmonic language is essentially nontraditional. Fourths, frequently in combination with seconds, are prominent, reflected in the open-fifth sonorities of the two main cadences (mm. 10 and 24). The cadences are defined by linear progression rather than traditional harmonic means—by the resolution of the lower leading tone in the top voice (C♯–D and F♯–G, respectively) and the "upper" leading tone in the bass (D♯–D and G♯–G, slightly elaborated).

Example 1 sketches the most important linear and intervallic relationships.[1] The two main sections are divided into four subphrases marked I*a*, I*b*, II*a*, and II*b*: mm. 1–4, 5–10, 11–18, 19–24. The end of I*a* is defined by the arrival on B♭⁵ of the soprano (m. 4), the goal of the melodic-rhythmic motion so far, while the beginning of I*b* (mm. 5–10) coincides with the bass's arrival on C♯³, the leading tone for the first cadence at m. 10 and the tonal focus for mm. 5–9. (C♯ is maintained—or "prolonged"—both by the bass's C♯-minor triad, outlined on the downbeats of mm. 5–8, and by the top voice's repeated returns to C♯ at mm. 5.4, 6.4, 8.2, and 9.4.) The introduction of a new falling melodic figure in m. 5, repeated and varied in mm. 6 and 7–8, also supports the grouping of subphrases.

EXAMPLE 1

I*b* returns transposed up a perfect fourth but otherwise unaltered as II*b*, mm. 19–24, the second subphrase of the second half (conforming to a common binary procedure). II*a* presents more developmental, contrasting material, reaching a climax at m. 16, followed by a two-measure "cadenza" that releases energy before the return. The length of the four subphrases expands to the climax, then contracts for the return: 4 + 6 + 8 + 6.

The harmonic progression of the climactic section is controlled by sequential repetitions of descending minor-third arpeggiations, derived from the bass's C♯-minor arpeggiation in mm. 5–8 (also, more freely but closer to the sur-

1.   For more detailed linear analyses of the Interlude, which differ in significant respects with the present one as well as with each other, see Felix Salzer, *Structural Hearing* (New York, 1952), vol. 1, p. 329, and vol. 2, pp. 274–77; and David Neumeyer, *The Music of Paul Hindemith* (New Haven, 1986), pp. 49–53 and 75–81.

face, from the top voice of mm. 5, 6, and 7–8). The bass descends triadically to E^2 (m. 12), $G\sharp^2$ (m. 14), and C^2 (m. 15.4); and, as did the lowest pitch of the C♯ arpeggio, each of these pitches proceeds by half step: E to D♯ (mm. 12–13), G♯ to G (m. 14), and C to B (mm. 15.4–16), the last B supplying the bass of the climactic chord. The top voice simultaneously rises—also triadically—to C^6 (m. 16), eclipsing the previous B^5 of mm. 5–7. It then rises during the cadenza through $D\flat^6$ (m. 17.1, anticipated by $D\flat^7$ in m. 16) to $D\sharp^6$ (m. 18.4).

$D\sharp^6$, enharmonically a perfect fourth higher than the $B\flat^5$ in m. 4, resolves as did that note by a half step upward, initiating the transposed repetition of mm. 5–10. The F♯ in the bass at m. 19 (corresponding to C♯ in m. 5) grows out of the climactic B triad, replacing F♮ in mm. 16–18 (the F-F♯ exchange is anticipated in the middle voice of the parallel-chord succession, mm. 16.6–17).

The exposition of *Fuga tertia,* a three-voice fugue, follows tradition: the soprano, bass (m. 7), and tenor (m. 13) enter one by one with statements of the subject on the tonic, submediant (rather than the traditional dominant), and tonic (initially obscured by the bass's D♭ in m. 13, a typical fugal practice). A strong tonic cadence also closes the exposition at m. 19.1.

Here too, tonal definition depends on linear rather than harmonic matters. Thus the subject moves up by thirds from F^4, the tonic, to $E\flat^5$ (combined with a characteristic fourth sequence, G-C / B♭-E♭, in m. 2), and then descends mainly by step to F^4 again (Example 2). The submediant answer (m. 7) is deflected back toward F in its last measure through $A\flat^3$ and $G\flat^3$ (m. 12). The return to F is underlined by the soprano, which moves repeatedly between F^4 and C^5 in mm. 13–15 and on to F^5 at m. 17, before falling to its cadential A^4.

EXAMPLE 2

The first episode (which contains no subject, mm. 19–23) modulates from F to A, the bass deliniating the motion with an essentially stepwise descent to A^3 (mm. 19.3–23.1) as the soprano repeats a figure recalling the similarly repeating soprano figure from mm. 5–6 and 20–21 of the Interlude. The cadence on A (m. 23.1) overlaps with the beginning of a new expository section in that key; an inverted statement of the subject appears in the soprano, later joined by an uninverted statement in the bass (m. 24.3), leading to a second A cadence (m. 30.1).

From m. 30.4 to the end the music is an exact retrograde of mm. 1–30.1. This seemingly mechanical procedure works well here owing to the structure of the first half. Since the subject outlines a roughly symmetrical linear shape, from F^4 to $E\flat^5$ and back, it remains essentially unchanged when played backward (as does the almost steady rhythm). The overall tonal-formal plan also lends itself to reversal. An extended expository section in the tonic (mm. 1–19.1) followed by an episode modulating to the mediant (mm. 19.2–23.1) and a brief expository section in the new key (mm. 23.1–30.1) produce, when reversed, a second brief expository section in the mediant (mm. 30.4–37.1), a modulatory episode back to the home key (mm. 37.2–41.3), and an extended final exposition in the tonic (mm. 41.4–59). The only change is that the tenor and bass do not drop out at mm. 48 and 54 (which would correspond to their entrances in the first half), the full three-voice texture being maintained to the end.

17

ROGER SESSIONS (1896–1985)
from *From My Diary* (1940)

a. No. 2

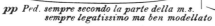

b. No. 3

ANALYTICAL COMMENTS

Sessions was moving away from the Stravinsky-influenced neo-classicism of his earlier style when he wrote these two pieces, whose chromaticism, constant thematic development, and intensely contrapuntal conception reflect an increasing attraction to the Schoenberg orbit. Yet certain "classicizing" elements, to which Sessions always remained committed, persist: consistent textures, strongly etched thematic profiles, and unambiguous formal outlines. The chromaticism, while avoiding triadic harmonies or functional progression, remains in some sense tonal, with fixed pitch configurations recurring at prominent points, yet in neither piece producing an unequivocal "center." Moreover, despite Sessions's conscious rejection of "vernacularisms," there is an unmistakably "American" quality about the music, especially evident in the syncopated shifting of duplet and triplet groupings in No. 2.

The second piece falls into three sections, mm. 1–29, 30–50, and 51–71, the outer ones characterized by a fast tempo and aggressive forward propulsion, the middle by a slower tempo and more lyrical disposition. The opening half-step motive in the right hand is a kind of basic "motto" for the piece. Repeated in m. 3, it is spun out into a longer melodic succession that reaches a temporary goal on F^4 at m. 5.2, extending the chromatic motion initiated by the opening G^4-$F\sharp^4$. (Such linear connections are critical in Sessions and partly account for the music's quasi-tonal character.) The association of F with the opening motive actually goes back to mm. 1 and 3, where the rising left-hand figure moves from G^1 (doubling the right hand) to a repeated F^2-$A\flat^2$ figure that, together with the motto, fills out the chromatic aggregate F-$A\flat$.

Although at first glance the left hand seems essentially figurative and accompanimental, it proves to be as motivically and linearly conceived as the right. The left hand's complementary rhythmic relationship with the right hand enables it to undertake its own development beneath the long right-hand F$\sharp$ in m. 2, introducing the perfect fourth (and its inversion, the perfect fifth), an interval that becomes increasingly important in the upper part as well. Following the arrival on F^4 in m. 5, the right hand joins the left in a texturally heightened, rising version of the idea from m. 2. And when the right hand returns to octaves (m. 7.4), it continues with rising fourths, eventually combining them with falling chromatic seconds (m. 9). This leads to the first climax (m. 10.1), on an octave-doubled F^7 that continues the pattern of rising octaves begun at m. 7.4; the climax is punctuated by the left hand with its own rising fourth–falling second figure (m. 10.1), closing with the initial G-F$\sharp$. This concludes the first formal unit of the first section, whose most important pitch relationships are summarized in Example 1.

Following a three-measure transition and dissolution, the longer second unit opens in m. 13, a free development and extension of material from the

EXAMPLE 1

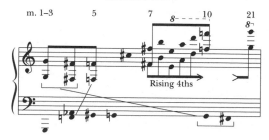

first. It begins with varied statements of the right- and left-hand figures from mm. 1–2 and continues with a corresponding rising motion that leads to a climactic octave-doubled G^7 in m. 21, connecting linearly with the climactic F^7 from m. 10. (This G also supplies the previously withheld extension of the rising fourth sequence from mm. 7–9; see Example 1.) Instead of breaking off abruptly as before, this second climax is brought down gradually in a longer transition (mm. 22–29). The final notes in the right hand, $G\flat^2$-$F\flat^2$, reiterate a major-second version of the opening idea (compare m. 13).

This final $G\flat$-$F\flat$ is filled in by the F^2 that opens the middle section, part of a return of the F-A$\flat$ figure, radically transformed in character. The right hand also opens on F (F^3) and then continues to E^4 and $G\flat^4$, repeating the pitches that ended the previous section and producing a new development of the original half-step idea. The middle section, building to the climax at m. 47, proceeds as if in a single breath. The long right-hand line is articulated into subphrases by references at mm. 37 and 43 to the rising figure of m. 30; both references are preceded by rests, and the second is compressed to a single eighth note as the music pushes toward the climax. A brief transition following the climax in m. 47 leads back to the return of the first section at m. 51.

The reprise is completely rethought and considerably compressed. The opening gesture is transposed and otherwise varied. The main climax (mm. 60–61) restates the rising fourth idea but reinforces it with three-note chords rather than octaves. And the final cadence brings back the content of the opening gesture at its original pitch level: G-F$\sharp$ in the right hand, F-A$\flat$ in the left. The final resolution this provides is strengthened by a strong linear attraction from the $A\flat^4$-G^4 oscillations of the dissolution in mm. 67–68 to the final G^4-$F\sharp^4$.

The third piece shares certain materials with the second (all four pieces in the set are interrelated) and similarly opens with G-F$\sharp$, now expressed as a simultaneous, grace-note-inflected minor ninth. The ninth is repeated, unchanged, until m. 5.3, when it breaks away and rises to a high point at m. 8 before falling back quickly to its original position (m. 9), which is then maintained to the end. The F$\sharp$-G configuration thus forms a relatively stable nucleus around which the other elements orient themselves.

There are two additional components: the melodic idea introduced in the left hand at m. 1.3 transforms the chromatic idea into a complete neighbor-note figure (transposed), followed by a leap upward to a closing gesture; and a two-note version of the chromatic figure in the right hand, introduced at m. 2.2 and placed registrally within the minor-ninth configuration, rhythmically complements and echoes the pitches of the left's neighbor idea. After a restatement in m. 3, the left-hand idea begins to develop as the right-hand echo loses its rhythmic independence, becoming attached to the minor ninth. The left hand intensifies rhythmically and moves upward, helping build to the climax in m. 8, which it punctuates with an emphatic, rhythmically augmented statement of the falling-second motive from m. 2. When the minor-ninth configuration falls back to its original position, the left hand follows with a final, simplified and eventually augmented statement of the neighbor idea at the original pitch level.

The piece thus sets out a limited and relatively stable set of relationships at the opening, departs from them to develop to a point of maximum tension, and returns to them before closing. The overall shape, defined by register, rhythmic intensification, tempo, and dynamics, is unusually clear. The key signature, however, presents something of a puzzle. According to friends and former students, Sessions considered the piece to be in B minor. Yet B plays no explicitly significant role (it does not even appear until mm. 7–8, and then only briefly in an inner voice), so that its centricity seems tenuous at best. (B is perhaps implied by the F♯-G configuration, functioning as a quasi-dominant.) A more likely choice of key would seem to be D♯ major-minor, since D♯ (root) and F♯ and G (minor and major thirds) of D♯-major-minor are heavily emphasized in both opening and closing measures, with the root positioned in the bass, decorated by the leading tone. (The fifth of the triad also appears prominently in mm. 2–3, spelled B♭.) Yet in such chromatic music it is probably better not to try to pin down a key in any traditional sense suggesting functional tonality, but to consider the "tonic" as an artificial, nontriadic, and contextually defined structural focus, whose tonal implications are necessarily ambiguous.

handwritten annotations:
- right hand, chords
- left hand, strumming
- really forward looking

18

HENRY COWELL (1897–1965)
Piano Pieces *westcoast; Asian*

a. *Aeolian Harp* (1923)

strings in box → activated by the wind

Explanation of Symbols

All of the notes of the "Aeolian Harp" should be pressed down on the keys, without sounding, at the same time being played on the open strings of the piano with the other hand.

sw. indicates that the strings should be swept from the lowest to the highest note of the chord given, or if the arpeggio mark is given with a downward arrow, from the top to the bottom note of the chord.

pizz. indicates the string is to be plucked. Both sweeps and plucks are made with the flesh of the finger unless otherwise indicated.

"inside" indicates that the notes are to be played near the center of the string, inside the steel bar which runs parallel to the keyboard across the strings.

"outside" indicates that the notes are to be played outside this bar, near the tuning pegs.

Except where indicated, the pedal must NEVER BE DOWN while the strings are being swept; as soon as the sweep is made, the pedal should be put down, and held until the time is ready to begin a new sweep, when it must be released.

handwritten annotation: cadential area

b. *Fabric* (1917?)

Explanation of New Rhythms and Notes

In musical time a whole-note (**o**) is the unit by which all shorter time-values are measured, for instance an eighth-note (♪) is so called because it occupies one eighth the time of a whole-note; a quarter-note (♩) is so called because it occupies one quarter the time of a whole-note, etc.

The only regular system of subdividing a whole-note is by twos into halves, quarters, eighths, etc. If notes of other time values, for instance notes occupying one twelfth of a whole-note, are desired, they are called "eighth-note triplets" and written as eighth-notes, with a figure *3* over them, thus ♪♪♪. Why not call them twelfth-notes, as would seem natural?

It is here proposed that all these irregular time-values be called by their correct names, according to the part of a whole-note they occupy. Thus ♩♩♩ are third-notes instead of "half-note triplets" since each occupies one third of the time of a whole-note; ♩♩♩♩♩ are fifth-notes instead of "quarter-note quintuplets", etc.

Although heretofore not suggested in notation, it will be seen that third, sixth, twelfth and twenty-fourth-notes form a related series; fifth, tenth and twentieth-notes another, and in fact, that a new series can be formed on each odd number and its divisions by two.

A new notation which brings out these relationships will be used as follows:

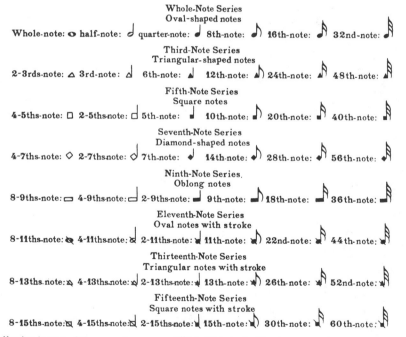

Whole-Note Series
Oval-shaped notes

Whole-note: **o** half-note: ♩ quarter-note: ♩ 8th-note: ♪ 16th-note: ♫ 32nd-note: ♬

Third-Note Series
Triangular-shaped notes

2-3rds-note: △ 3rd-note: ◭ 6th-note: ◮ 12th-note: ◮♪ 24th-note: ◮♫ 48th-note: ◮♬

Fifth-Note Series
Square notes

4-5ths-note: □ 2-5ths-note: ◻ 5th-note: ◼ 10th-note: ◼♪ 20th-note: ◼♫ 40th-note: ◼♬

Seventh-Note Series
Diamond-shaped notes

4-7ths-note: ◇ 2-7ths-note: ◈ 7th-note: ◆ 14th-note: ◆♪ 28th-note: ◆♫ 56th-note: ◆♬

Ninth-Note Series
Oblong notes

8-9ths-note: ▭ 4-9ths-note: ◻ 2-9ths-note: ▬ 9th-note: ▬ 18th-note: ▬♪ 36th-note: ▬♫

Eleventh-Note Series
Oval notes with stroke

8-11ths-note: ✧ 4-11ths-note: ✦ 2-11ths-note: ✦ 11th-note: ♪ 22nd-note: ♫ 44th-note: ♬

Thirteenth-Note Series
Triangular notes with stroke

8-13ths-note: ✕ 4-13ths-note: ✕ 2-13ths-note: ◮ 13th-note: ◮♪ 26th-note: ◮♫ 52nd-note: ◮♬

Fifteenth-Note Series
Square notes with stroke

8-15ths-note: ◼ 4-15ths-note: ◼ 2-15ths-note: ◼ 15th-note: ◼♪ 30th-note: ◼♫ 60th-note: ◼♬

Following is part of the second measure of "Fabric", in both old and new notation. It will be seen that the new notation saves the use of several tied tones, as well as figures and brackets.

OLD   NEW

Andante

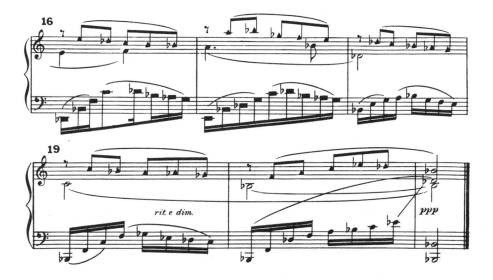

ANALYTICAL COMMENTS

These two compositions are representative of experimental piano pieces Cowell composed during the late 1910s and 1920s. *Aeolian Harp* is a study in sonority, one of several works in which Cowell exploited the possibilities of playing inside the piano, on the strings rather than the keyboard. Two methods of setting the strings into vibration are employed: sweeping the hand quickly across several strings, and plucking one string at a time (pizzicato). The sweeping motion is used with strings whose keys have been silently pressed, allowing them to vibrate freely. Thus, although the hand sweeps across all the strings between the lowest and highest notated pitches in the first chord (from D^{b4} to A^{b4}), only those pitches for which keys are pressed (D^b, F, and A^b) will sustain, while the others (D, E^b, E, G^b, and G) will be immediately dampened.

Formally the piece is quite simple. It is made up of a series of four similar half-note chord progressions using triads and seventh chords exclusively, the end of each progression marked by a pizzicato arpeggiation of the final chord. The first three progressions are distinguished by dynamics, direction of sweeping, and—in part of the third—arpeggiation with thumbnail rather than flesh of the finger. The final progression repeats the first exactly.

The four progressions are linked by a succession of perfect-fifth and tritone root connections joining beginnings and endings of phrases (Example 1). In addition, the highest notes of the progressions and the top notes of

EXAMPLE 1

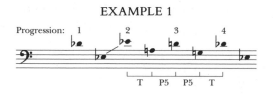

the pizzicato arpeggiations connect linearly with one another, either by repetition or by step, producing the succession shown in Example 2.

EXAMPLE 2

Fabric, though composed earlier, is a more complex piece, reflecting Cowell's interest in new rhythmic structures.[1] Each strand of the three-part texture divides a basic unit of time (equal to the notated 2/4 measure) differently. Rather than using standard duple and triple divisions, Cowell employs subdivisions of 5, 6, 7, 8, and 9, and rather than notating these in the cumbersome traditional manner with brackets and numbers, he uses a specially devised notation, explained in a preface to the score.

Each of the three strands has its own rhythmic structure. The bottom voice subdivides by 8 and 9, the middle voice by 5, and the top voice by 6 and 7. Each also has its own register and function, with the middle voice—marked at a higher dynamic level—containing the principal melodic line. The middle voice is also the only one to maintain a constant unit of subdivision and to present consistently differentiated groupings of the subdivision. The bottom voice has the bass, always on the downbeat, plus a figurational pattern consisting primarily of arpeggiations. The top voice supplies a filigree-like appendage to the principal line; it begins every measure with a rest that allows the main voice to attack its first note without upper-voice competition, and usually continues with an upper-octave doubling of that note.

Except for rhythm, the texture is thus essentially "normal," illustrating Cowell's penchant for combining highly innovative elements with traditional ones. Even the rhythmic effect is softened by the lowest voice's use of duple subdivision (by eight) in the opening and closing measures. Indeed, this sounds rather like a slightly out-of-focus version of a type of piano texture much favored by composers in the nineteenth and early twentieth centuries (e.g., Chopin and Skryabin).

The pitch structure offers a succession of triadically based harmonies, similarly thrown out of kilter by chromatic additions. The first two measures thus suggest a functional progression that moves deceptively by half-step bass motion, from C dominant seventh to B♭ minor in first inversion. B♭ minor is also the final chord to which the piece resolves, its root having been maintained as a pedal bass throughout the last four measures while the principal voice descended by step, one note per measure, from the third to the root. The main line moreover tends to suggest B♭ minor throughout.

1.   Rhythm is treated at considerable length in Cowell's pioneering theoretical study *New Musical Resources* (New York, 1930). Subdivisions of a basic durational unit, particularly relevant to this composition, are discussed on pp. 49–66.

Although the rhythmic structure of the piece is essentially continuous in effect, several veiled repetitions provide shape and coherence. Mm. 1–2 reappear only slightly altered in mm. 15–16, and there are several varied recurrences within the principal line alone; compare mm. 5–6 and 13–14, mm. 4–5 and 17–19, and mm. 1–2 and 9 (where the reference is rhythmically compressed and transposed).

19

AARON COPLAND (1900–1990)

Rodeo (1942), "Hoedown"

© Copyright 1946 by Aaron Copland; Copyright Renewed. Reprinted by permission of
Aaron Copland, Copyright Owner and Boosey & Hawkes, Inc., Sole Agents.

Intro – vamp – A – B – vamp – A'
(trans).

– borrowed tune – Bonaparte?
– barn dance music → collected in Kentucky in 1937

Picc.
a2
Flts. I & II
a2
Oboes I & II
C.A.
a2
Clts. I & II in B♭
Bass Clt. in B♭
Bsns I & II
I & II
Hns. in F
III & IV
I
Tpts. in B♭
II & III
Trombs. I & II
B.Tromb. & Tuba
Timp.
Tria.
Vln. I
Vln. II
Vla.
'Cello
Bass

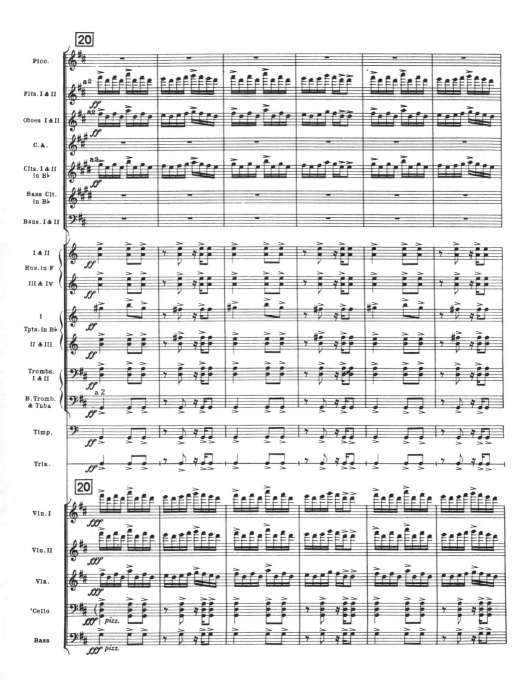

borrowed folk songs (western)

Coda

ANALYTICAL COMMENTS

The ballet *Rodeo* is representative of music Copland wrote during the later 1930s and 1940s in a more public, "democratic" style intended for broader audiences. It draws upon popular American materials and includes quotations from several cowboy songs. The "Hoe-Down" segment is a self-enclosed portion of the ballet.[1] Its principal thematic material is taken entirely from the barn-dance tune "Bonyparte,"[2] and the music is in general permeated with allusions to the type of "fiddle music" indigenous to the festive square dance gatherings known in the American West as hoedowns. Copland integrates these materials within a convincing symphonic context, transforming them yet retaining enough of their original character to project a distinctly popular image.

Dance forms typically have an additive structure, consisting of essentially separate numbers strung together in longer successions, and "Hoe-Down" accordingly contains a relatively large number of short, well-defined segments (usually eight measures in length), most of which return later, essentially unaltered. They are placed however, within a well-formed three-part design:

Introduction-*A* (rn 5–11)-*B* (rn 12–18)-*A'* (rn 19–22)[3]

Tonally, the introduction and *A* sections are firmly anchored in D, while the *B* section opens in G and then moves on to A.

The introduction begins with a preparatory four-measure segment based on turns around the tonic D, accompanied by syncopated D repetitions; this is followed by a similarly introductory fanfarelike statement of D-major brass arpeggiations with string syncopations in a series of open fifths evoking the sound of fiddlers tuning. The opening segment returns (rn 2), now followed by a "vamp" (beginning one measure before rn 3)—an introductory section in which a standard accompanimental figure is reiterated before the melody enters. One humorous aspect of this vamp is that it turns out not to be accompanimental: it never acquires a melody, and returns later as an independent idea.[4] Another results from the oddly syncopated offbeat sixteenth notes in the fourth measure of the vamp, and from the "short-limbed" three-measure group beginning three measures before rn 4 (exaggerated in the repetitions of this group at rn 4 and four measures later by rests on the downbeats of the third measure of each group).

1.   This segment forms one of the excerpts chosen by the composer for the orchestral suite *Rodeo: Four Dance Episodes* (also 1942), and was rescored as an independent work for string orchestra in 1945.
2.   The tune can be found in John A. and Alan Lomax's *Our Singing Country* (New York, 1941), 54–55.
3.   In this discussion, the designation rn refers to rehearsal number, as notated in the score.
4.   Here one sees Copland's Stravinskian tendency—most readily evident, ironically, in his populist works—to treat "borrowed" materials in a fragmentary, dislocated manner.

When the turn figure reappears at rn 5, opening the first *A* section, it represents the initial measure of a complete statement of the tune "Bonyparte," which supplies all of this section's melodic material. The tune contains two eight-measure units: *x* (rn 5) and *y* (rn 6). Its syncopated quality, emphasized in Copland's setting, recalls the introduction, as do the accompanimental open fifths in *y*. When "Bonyparte" is repeated at rn 7, the *y* segment is altered: the melody is an octave lower than before, a new, rhythmically active pedal D is added in the horns, and the scoring changes when the four-measure subphrase is repeated. These changes prove significant when, instead of returning to *x* as before, *y* is restated in an orchestrally expanded version (rn 9), which is thus heard as the culmination of a larger process of orchestral development spanning the entire repeat of the borrowed tune. The previous syncopations turn into the brass's syncopated "pedal" at rn 9, a massive, simultaneous version of the open-fifth idea extending upward from G through D and A to E.

After this climactic moment the *x* segment of the tune returns once more, now in a transitional role. At first unaltered (rn 10), it is broken up through motivic dissolution after two measures when repeated (rn 11, the first time *x* has been altered in any way). The introductory turn reappears (four measures before rn 12) and is also dissolved, leading to the *B* section. Despite its repetitions, *A* thus builds to a single climax, followed by a brief transition.

The *B* section is set off through lighter scoring and more active harmonic motion. During the first eight-measure segment (rn 12), its opening G-major tonality (stabilizing a pitch heard several times in the *A* section as the lowest note of open-fifth combinations) moves from G to A. The second segment (rn 13) remains in a modally tinged A minor, accompanied by a progression in open fifths that moves more independently in rhythm and root succession than the essentially static "tuning" fifths of the *A* section it recalls. The first segment returns at rn 14, orchestrally expanded to lead to the most active and developmental music of the entire piece (rn 15), climaxing with an eight-measure A-major segment (rn 16) that mimics the fiddling character in a considerably more elaborate texture. Violas, doubled by horns and trumpets in alternation, present an independent countermelody over a bass line that is more active than anywhere else in the piece. After a brief cadential extension (four measures before rn 17), somewhat reminiscent of the introductory fanfare, the vamp returns to provide a transition, fractured into a series of chromatically descending major triads sinking slowly from D to E♭ (rn 18 to two measures before rn 19).

The repeat of the *A* section (whose opening turn figure brings the preceding E♭ back to D) is significantly abridged, although all but the last two segments that return are unchanged. Table 1 aligns the two sections for comparison (*x* and *y* indicate the basic formal units, the numbers in parentheses their measure lengths).

While the music preceding *x'* is reduced by more than half (from forty-

TABLE 1

A: $x(8)-y(8)-x(8)-y(8)-y'(8)-x(8)-x'(7)$ + transition (4)
A': $x(8)-y(4)-y'(8)$ $x'(10)$ + coda (6)

eight measure to twenty), the final x' (rn 21) is lengthened and expanded in orchestration and registration, leading to a six-measure cadential flourish almost entirely on the pitch D (the only exception is the F♯ in the next-to-last measure, which brings back one of the piece's most prominent motives). The buildup to the climactic y' segment thus occurs much more quickly than before, while the x' that follows (which now does so immediately since the x segment formerly preceding it is omitted) abandons its former transitional function and drives on to a rousing finish.

20

ELLIOTT CARTER (b. 1908)
A Mirror on Which to Dwell (1975), "Argument"

Reprinted by arrangement with G. Schirmer / AMP.

1 Days that cannot bring you near
2 or will not,
3 Distance trying to appear
4 something more than obstinate,
5 argue argue argue with me
6 endlessly
7 neither proving you less wanted nor less dear.

8 Distance: Remember all that land
9 beneath the plane;
10 that coastline
11 of dim beaches deep in sand
12 stretching indistinguishably
13 all the way,
14 all the way to where my reasons end?

15 Days: And think
16 of all those cluttered instruments,
17 one to a fact,
18 canceling each other's experience;
19 how they were
20 like some hideous calendar
21 "Compliments of Never & Forever, Inc."

22 The intimidating sound
23 of these voices
24 we must separately find
25 can and shall be vanquished:
26 Days and Distance disarrayed again
27 and gone
28 both for good and from the gentle battleground.

ANALYTICAL COMMENTS

Argument is the second in a set of six settings by Carter of poems by the American poet Elizabeth Bishop for soprano and a chamber ensemble of nine instruments. Each song uses a different instrumental combination drawn from the complete ensemble—in this case, alto flute, bass clarinet, bongos, piano, cello, and double bass.

The main conceit of Bishop's poem—images of temporal and physical separation ("Days" and "Distance") as reflections of the personal alienation dividing two lovers—is musically projected by a texture featuring opposed and sharply contrasting components. More specifically, Bishop's metaphor of the "instruments" of interpersonal conflict, accumulating "one to a fact" like the days of a calendar, is embodied in the individualized writing for three different textural units, each asserting itself as a distinct personality within the larger group.

The overall structure of the poem follows the opposition of time and space—of lover against lover—in a larger rhythm that culminates in the climactic opening of the last of the four seven-lined verses: "The intimidating sound / of these voices." The first verse moves from the realm of "Days" (line 1) to that of "Distance" (line 3), while the second and third verses each focus exclusively on only one of the two images. This four-phased progression is articulated by verbal signals announcing the beginning of each unit: "Days" (line 1), "Distance" (line 3), "Distance" (line 8), "Days" (line 15). The pattern is broken at the first line of the final verse, after which the poem offers a suggestion of reconciliation. "Days" and "Distance" return to introduce the final unit (line 26), but here they are joined for the first time, and "disarrayed" as the lovers leave their "gentle battleground."

The formal and dynamic curve of Carter's music follows the verbal structure closely. This is especially evident in the vocal part, which provides a thread of continuity that faithfully traces the narrative line (distinguishing this piece from Carter's instrumental music, which normally does not reveal a single, central strand). Bishop's recurring verbal markers are associated throughout with the same pitches—"Days" with $G\sharp^4$ (mm. 6, 26, 39) and "Distance" with B^4 (mm. 8, 16, 40). These two pitches recur at other formal junctures, supplying anchors for the entire vocal line. Both appear in the setting of the thrice-stated "argue" that begins the last segment of the first verse (m. 10); B^4 closes the second verse (m. 23) and also appears prominently several times within that verse (mm. 18–20, 22); and $G\sharp^4$ is heard seven times at the close of the third verse (mm. 32–33).

The textual intensification as the final verse approaches is mirrored in a rising line formed by the highest pitches of the voice, moving upward from G^5 (m. 7) in the first verse to A^5 (m. 19) and $A\sharp^5$ (m. 22) in the second, back to A^5 in the third (three times in mm. 29–32), and finally culminating on the sustained B^5 accompanying "sound" near the opening of the last verse (m. 35), the highest vocal pitch in the piece.

The instrumental forces form three essentially independent textural layers of three different instrument types: winds (alto flute and bass clarinet), percussion (bongos and piano), and strings (cello and bass). Each unit has its own musical character, set off from the others by rhythm, texture, and pitch, and each has its own role within the larger texture. The winds are closely associated with the vocal line, at times seeming to provide a sort of unusually free heterophonic elaboration, as in their close interaction with the voice's $G\sharp$'s in mm. 6–7. (All the critical $G\sharp$'s and B's associated with "Days" and "Distance," in fact, are underscored by such heterophonic doublings.) At other moments the wind and voice connections are more fleeting, as in the winds' sustained $B\flat^3$-D^3 in mm. 12–13, which anticipates the $B\flat^4$-D^4 in the voice at the end of m. 13. Only as the climax nears does the wind layer begin to break away from the voice more completely.

The string unit resembles the winds in that it too mimics the vocal line, though less consistently. Thus the cello's $G\sharp^4$ in m. 4 anticipates the voice's opening G#^{4} in m. 6, and its B^4 in mm. 7–8 anticipates the voice's B^4 on "Distance" in m. 8. This string unit projects its independence sooner, however, particularly the bass, which beginning in m. 8 offers a sort of lumbering, intermittent countermelody to the voice.

Finally, the percussion group interjects commentaries based on rapid quintuplet and nonuplet divisions, with frequent note and note-group repetitions in the piano complementing the fixed registral alternations of the bongos. The percussion's persistent "clatter" provides a vivid sonic analogue for the "argument" of the poem.

Rhythmically and texturally, the three instrumental layers work independently of one another throughout most of the song, alternating and overlapping in staggered cycles before they finally begin to coalesce as the climax approaches. (An interesting feature is the way the instrumental components, so dissociated from the voice line in other ways, connect with it through the previously mentioned pitch doublings.) The maximum interpenetration occurs in mm. 31–32, the textural climax. Not only do all three accompanimental layers completely overlap here for the first time, they take on an essentially unified character; both winds and strings temporarily assume the personality of the percussion layer, echoing the percussion's characteristic repeating figures and the bongos' quintuplet rhythmic divisions.

This instrumental climax does not coincide with the vocal-poetic one but immediately precedes it, at the "hideous calendar" of mutual rejections. Following this moment of maximum overlapping, the percussion drops out, allowing the voice to soar up relatively unencumbered to its climactic B^5, accompanied by a greatly simplified instrumental component (played at a relatively loud dynamic level, however).

The reconciliation suggested in the poem's final verse is reflected musically in a gradual decrease in the accompaniment's textural density and dynamic level (though Carter seems to underscore the difficulty of reconciliation by letting the percussion figures persist to the end). Especially emblematic is the "dispersion" of the two winds to their outer registral extremes after the voice completes its final phrase (mm. 47.4–50.1). The strings close with a group of six pitches identical to those presented at the opening of the piece by winds and strings (only the flute's opening C is missing). This six-pitch group, which contains both of the critical recurring pitches, G# and B, plays an important role in the piece; it returns complete in the winds and strings at m. 7.4, articulating the end of the first vocal phrase as well as the beginning of the second. A closely related pitch group also appears at m. 12.3, with the important G#-B component sustained until the end of the first verse (m. 14), and another related group appears at m. 17, marking the beginning the second verse.[1]

---

1. For a brief consideration of additional features of the pitch structure, see David Schiff, *The Music of Elliott Carter* (New York, 1983), pp. 288–89.

21

JOHN CAGE (b. 1912)
TV Köln (1958)

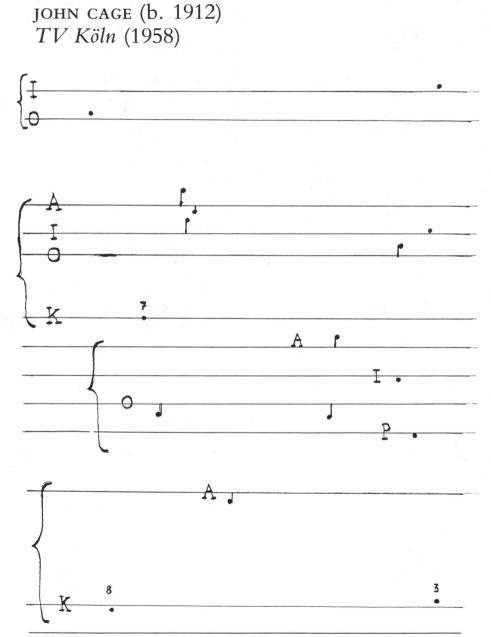

4 SYSTEMS OF EQUAL TIME LENGTH.

I = INTERIOR PIANO CONSTRUCTION
O = EXTERIOR ˝ ˙
A = AUXILIARY NOISE
K = KEYBOARD (NUMBERS = NO. OF KEYS)
POSITION OF NOTE WITH RESPECT TO LINE
GIVES RELATIVE PITCH. DURATION OR AMPLITUDE

ANALYTICAL COMMENTS

Although Cage began incorporating chance operations in the composition of his music during the early 1950s, the pitches and overall time frame of his music written during the years immediately following remained more or less precisely specified. *TV Köln,* written near the end of the 1950s, was one of his first works to introduce indeterminacy into the area of performance.

The score consists of a single page containing four systems of notation, preceded by a page of instructions. The instructions indicate that the systems are of equal duration, but do not specify an actual duration. In principle, the piece could thus last from a few seconds to virtually any length, although given the limited number of notated events, a relatively brief performance is perhaps more likely. The instructions also explain the four letters associated with the lines of the systems. These lines, unlike the staves of traditional piano music, do not separate bass and treble clef, or right hand and left hand, but distinguish the type of sound played or—more accurately—where that sound is produced: on the keys (K), inside the piano (I), on the piano's exterior surface (O), or somewhere other than the piano (A). The only additional information provided is that a note's position with respect to a line may indicate either its relative pitch, relative duration, or relative amplitude.

These instructions refer not so much to the particular sounds to be played (a partial exception being the number of keys pressed for keyboard events) as to the way the sounds are to be produced. What is indicated are essentially actions, not musical events. *TV Köln* is thus not a musical composition in any conventional sense, but a sort of generalized frame for constructing sonic and temporal relationships. As Cage himself has consistently maintained, he is interested not in creating "works of art," but in providing contexts within which performers can carry out various types of activities, and within which any type of sound can have as much, or as little, significance as any other. The "music" only results from the experience of performing, which varies each time the score is realized.

The instructions leave considerable room for choice. Absolute durations between events, as we have seen, are completely indeterminate; and a single

notational parameter, the placement of notes relative to lines, covers three
independent variables (relative pitch, duration, and amplitude), thereby
leaving all three largely at the performer's disposal. The variability of the
specific sonic events chosen ranges from the exact distribution of keyboard
notes to the choice of "auxiliary noises," which might be virtually any-
thing. The difference between stemmed and unstemmed note heads is not
explained (the former are apparently used in ambiguous cases to indicate the
line to which an event is attached), nor is the meaning of the P on the fifth
line of the third system (where one would expect a K).

Despite these uncertainties, however, *TV Köln* has a definite "shape,"
because the events that constitute it have been arranged in a given temporal
relationship with one another. This shape even has, however inadvertently,
a certain traditional quality. The piece opens with a single isolated event;
continues (from the end of the first system) with a relatively quick succession of events that reaches maximum density at the end of the third system
(the sequence of event groupings in this succession is 1-3-2-1-4-1, the final
1 being the keyboard event at the beginning of the fourth system); and
closes with two more isolated events, separated by increasing lengths of
silence.

Soon after composing *TV Köln,* in order to avoid such evocations (no
doubt unintended) of "imposed" conventional structure as well as to pre-
vent *any* structure from being permanently attached to a composition, Cage
began a series of pieces notated on unbound, transparent sheets containing
lines, dots, and circles (these pieces were entitled Variations). For the works
to be realized, the sheets must be superimposed by the performers, who
arrange them according to their own inclinations, so that, unlike the present
work, which has a single, "hard" score, the form as well as content varies
with each new realization.

22

BENJAMIN BRITTEN (1913–76)
Peter Grimes (1945), Interlude IV and Act II,
Scene 2

Interlude IV

Music by Benjamin Britten; Libretto by Montague Slater. © Copyright 1945 by Boosey &
Hawkes, Ltd.; Copyright Renewed. Reprinted by permission of Boosey & Hawkes, Inc.

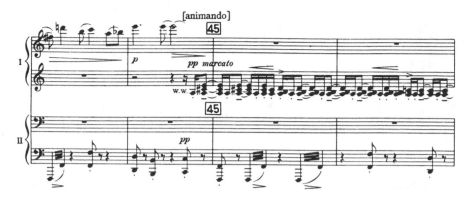

Scene II. Peter Grimes' hut (an upturned boat .... ~ —

with one door, left, opening to the path from the Borough, and another, back centre, to the cliff with a way down to the sea)—
later the same morning. The boy staggers through the path door as if thrust from behind. Peter follows in a towering rage.

61 Adagio (♪ = 66)

storm.   And she will   soon for-get her school-house ways   For-get the

la-bour of those weary days   Wrapp'd round............ in kind - ness   like September

haze.   The learn-ed   at their books have no more store   Of wis-dom than we'd

close.............. be-hind our   door,   Com - par'd............ with us

the rich man would be... poor.   I've seen in... stars the life   that we might

con forza

P. ...... there is no stone In earth's thick - ness.......... to make a home,

sempre f

P. That you can build with.......... and re - main a - lone.

mf

Hobson's drum, at the head of the Borough procession, can be heard very distantly coming towards the hut. ___ Peter

64 Grave *(come sopra)*   Adagio   *con orrore*

P. Some-times I

HOBSON'S DRUM *(off)*

ppp   *senza espr.*   *ppp*

doesn't notice.

Grave   *ad lib. (senza voce)*

P. see that boy here in this hut. He's there now__ I can see him __ he is there!

H's. Drum

ppp

Adagio *(cantabile)*

P. His eyes... are..... on..... me...... as.... they.... were that e - - vil

ppp

Swallow draws the moral

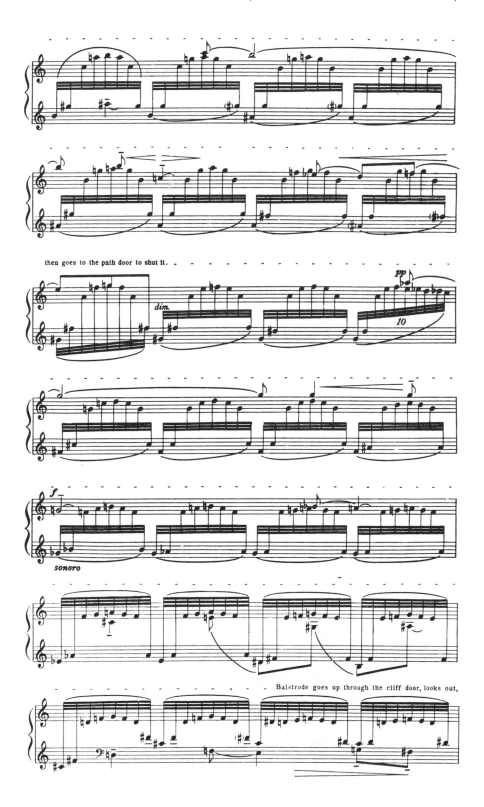

then goes to the path door to shut it.

Balstrode goes up through the cliff door, looks out,

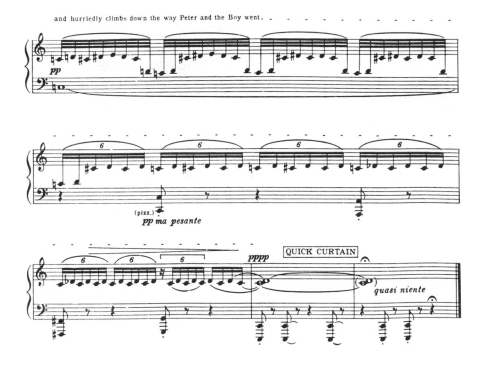

ANALYTICAL COMMENTS

Peter Grimes is set in an English fishing village. The title character, an outsider, is distrusted by the villagers because of his moodiness and bad temper, but he is also something of a dreamer and visionary. The opera deals with conflicts between society and the individual, and with the prejudices of the majority against those who fail to conform.

In a Prologue, Grimes is accused of having caused the death of his youthful apprentice at sea. Though the death is ruled accidental, most of the townspeople hold Grimes responsible. Only Captain Balstrode and Ellen, the village schoolmistress, support him. Events during the first act lead to the recruiting of a new apprentice for Grimes from a nearby orphanage.

The first scene of Act II takes place on a Sunday morning outside the village church. Ellen, having agreed to help look out for the new apprentice, notices a bruise on his neck. Grimes comes to take the boy on a fishing expedition; he has seen a great school of fish and hopes to win over the villagers with success. When Ellen protests that it is the Sabbath and inquires about the bruise, Grimes becomes angry, strikes her, and takes the boy away. A band of villagers determine to go to Grimes's hut and confront him.

The second scene is located in the hut. Like other scenes in the opera, it is preceded by an instrumental Interlude that is intimately tied to it, in this case a passacaglia.[1] The passacaglia theme, eleven beats in length, appears thirty-nine times, always unaltered (except in scoring) and always in the bass. (Because it has eleven beats, the theme occupies the same metrical position in the 4/4 measures only on every fourth occurrence.) It is derived from an idea associated with Grimes in the previous scene, sung—after he strikes Ellen—to the words "And God have mercy upon me!" and picked up by the villagers as they react to his violence ("Grimes is at his exercise!").

Since the variations differ in length (unlike those of a traditional passacaglia, where they correspond to single or multiple thematic statements), their beginnings and ends usually overlap, rather than coincide with, the theme. The first variation begins in the sixth measure of the Interlude, for example, after two unaccompanied theme statements, and the second begins after four and a half additional statements. There are eleven variations (the openings of each except the first are indicated in the score by rehearsal numbers), the second beginning at rn 45, the last at rn 54. Although apparently unfolding continuously, the variations are grouped by content and character (one plausible grouping is 1–3, 4–6, and 7–11). The final variations bring a noticeable intensification, especially from rn 51 on, culminating in the climactic chord that announces the opening of Scene 2 (rn 55).

The first variation conforms closely to the theme's tonal focus on F, but subsequent variations become more independent until the final one returns to F. Although essentially tonal and triadic, the music produces a clearly contemporary effect through the liberal use of chromatic inflections, shifting modal combinations, and nonfunctional progressions.

An important motive in the passacaglia comprises a descending minor third followed by a rising half step. Derived from notes 2–4 of the theme, it appears prominently in all the variations, often employed in a descending stepwise sequence spanning a falling perfect fifth (twice in the first variation: C^4 to F^3 six to ten measures after rn 44, E^4 to A^3 eleven to thirteen measures after rn 44). Such stepwise descents reappear in all variations until the ninth (rn 52), where an inverted form of the three-note motive initiates a rising line. One measure before the final, climactic variation (rn 54), original and inverted forms are combined. The passacaglia's recurrent theme and development of limited material suggest Grimes's tortured and obsessive character, and its growing intensity prepares for the brief, tragic scene that follows, the opera's dramatic climax.

Much of the scene's music is derived from the passacaglia; material from all variations except the second recurs in fragmentary, yet easily recognizable form. The scene alternates recitative and arioso sections, the recurring passacaglia fragments associated mainly with the former. Britten himself has referred to the "classical" nature of *Peter Grimes,* the "separate numbers that crystallize and hold the emotion of the dramatic situation at chosen

---

1.   The suite *Four Sea Interludes from Peter Grimes,* to which this passacaglia is often appended, is one of Britten's most frequently performed instrumental compositions.

moments." Yet the music moves in and out of these "numbers" so seamlessly that both dramatic and musical structure appear largely unbroken.

Grimes's cadenza-like "Go there!" (framed by prominent references to the three-note motive) announces his arrival at the hut and leads to a recitative section in which he tells the boy to prepare for fishing. During the first arioso (rn 58) Grimes dreams of his future in a moment of visionary fantasy (recapitulating music sung to similar words in Act I), his words trailing off at the end as he loses his train of thought. This passage is rooted entirely in D, mimicking the static quality of the passacaglia bass, and its prominent Lydian G♯ mirrors the theme's Lydian B.

In a second recitative Grimes again urges the boy to get ready. Thoughts of home and calm, treated more lyrically (rn 60), lead to an aria-like section (rn 61) with three strophic variations (seven, seven, and ten measures long). This music is also characterized by a raised fourth degree (here D♯) and static harmony (though each strophe ends with a sort of half cadence). And Grimes's vocal line revolves obsessively around the same pitches (C♯ and, less frequently, E) and melodic configurations.

The music that preceded the aria at rn 60 returns at rn 63 to introduce the aria's reprise (three measures after rn 64). Here, however, as Grimes's dreaming gives way to nightmarish hallucinations, the music is grotesquely distorted. With the Lydian D♯ now in the bass, tritone and chromatic relationships are emphasized; and the three strophes are radically fragmented (2 + 2 + 1 measures), interrupted by the sound of a drum accompanying the villagers to the hut.

The motivic integrity of this entire "aria" section stems from the expressive rising minor sixth and falling major second accompanying Grimes's "some kindlier home" (two measures after rn 60, repeated six measures after rn 60), which provide the principal accompanimental figure and the basis for the imitative music at the *Più animato* (seven measures after rn 63). These imitations funnel into a dissonant chord (rn 64), which accompanies the recurring drum figures and also provides the harmonic foundation for the distorted reprise. The chord disappears, one note at a time, when the villagers are first heard (three measures after rn 65).

The next segment (two measures after rn 65) cuts between the music of the villagers approaching the hut (their opening "Now!" rising diatonically stepwise at each reappearance, from G^4-C^4 three measures after rn 65 to D^5-G^4 three measures after rn 68) and the music accompanying Peter's frantic efforts to leave the cabin with the boy and get down the cliff to his boat. The villagers' material is drawn from the previous scene (heard as they prepared to set off after Grimes), while Grimes is accompanied by music from the passacaglia (rn 66), including an inverted and newly rhythmicized version of the complete bass theme that appears off and on until rn 69. The villagers' arrival at the hut (rn 69) is marked by another statement of their refrain, now a major third higher than before, and by the interruption of the accompaniment by a chromatic cluster comprising A♯, B, and C. After building dynamically and instrumentally to a tutti downbeat *(fffz)* four measures later, the cluster reduces to an eerie celesta arpeggio as the boy falls down the cliff to his death.

When the villagers enter they find nothing, leading the hypocritical Swallow (who has been largely responsible for the distrust of Grimes) to urge "less interference in our private lives" (rn 71, marked *pomposo*). The scene ends with a moving return to the music of the first passacaglia variation (rn 72), again played by solo viola but here inverted, plus a final restatement of the passacaglia theme (four measures from the end), now on C but otherwise unchanged. The celesta in the meantime has progressively lowered and contracted its arpeggiations until only C^4 and Db^4 remain.

23

MILTON BABBITT (b. 1916)
Semi-Simple Variations (1956)

ANALYTICAL COMMENTS

Despite its title, modest length, and early date, this piece provides an excellent example of the complexities of organization characteristic of all Babbitt's music. These remarks will focus mainly on the pitch structure and how it relates to the form of the movement.

The work is based on a twelve-tone row that appears in the top voice of mm. 1–12 (Example 1). In contrast to "classical" (Schoenbergian) twelve-tone procedures, this row is not used exclusively but rather serves as a source set from which other rows are derived. Indeed, the first hexachord of the basic row might itself be considered the true source set, since the second hexachord is its retrograde, transposed at the tritone.

EXAMPLE 1

Additional rows are based on manipulations of adjacent three-note groups ("trichords") drawn from this hexachord, of which there are four (labeled i, ii, iii, and iv in Example 2).

EXAMPLE 2

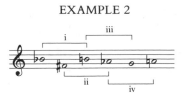

Each of these generates a derived set (labeled *A, B, C,* and *D* in Example 3).

EXAMPLE 3

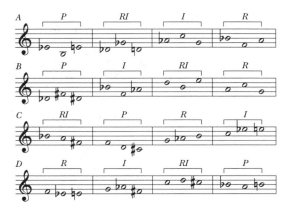

Each of these four rows consists entirely of forms of a single trichord, and each contains all four forms of that trichord (original, inversion, retrograde, and retrograde inversion), labeled *P, I, R,* and *RI* in the example.

A fifth row is derived from two trichords, ii and iii (labeled *E* in Example 4).

EXAMPLE 4

Finally, a sixth row is generated by reversing the order of the original row's two hexachords (labeled *P,* with an indication of hexachord reversal, in Example 5).

EXAMPLE 5

For compositional purposes, the source row and six derived rows are arranged into five four-voiced structures (Example 6).[1]

EXAMPLE 6

Each of the five structures consists of four simultaneous rows, producing four distinct voices differentiated by register, and each structure corresponds to a section of the piece, designated Variations I, II, III, IV, and V.

1. This table is similar to Example 2a in Christopher Wintle, "Milton Babbitt's *Semi-Simple Variations,*" *Perspectives of New Music,* 14–15 (1976): 128. Wintle's article offers a useful introduction to the theoretical foundation of Babbitt's music, with particular reference to this piece. (Babbitt has expressed reservations about the analysis of the rhythmic structure: see his "Responses: A First Approximation" in the same volume, p. 18.) Also recommended is Elaine Barkin, "A Simple Approach to Milton Babbitt's *Semi-Simple Variations,*" *The Music Review,* 28 (1967): 316–22.

Variation I comprises the first twelve measures of the piece, while each subsequent variation contains six measures. The divisions are thus: I (mm. 1–12), II (13–18), III (19–24), IV (25–30), and V (31–36).

An important aspect of the four-voiced structures concerns the aggregate organization. (An aggregate is any group of pitches containing all twelve pitches of the tempered scale, regardless of order.) Since each voice in each structure is a twelve-tone row, it is itself of course an aggregate. In addition, the rows are arranged so that vertical (or "harmonic") aggregates occur. Thus the first three vertical tetrachords (or four-part "chords") of each row, which result from the coincidence of the four voices, form a twelve-tone aggregate, as do tetrachords 4–6, 5–8, and 9–12. (This grouping by threes reinforces the trichordal structure of the derived rows.) In addition, the two upper hexachords of each half structure form an aggregate, as do the two lower hexachords.

The five four-part structures in Example 6 represent not compositional content but an abstract framework that is transformed through the actual events of the piece—there is no succession of choral-like four-part chords. The structures are both rhythmically and texturally varied, with significant changes occurring between sectional divisions (though registral differentiation distinguishes the four voices in all five). Both the order and octave of the pitches are fixed, however, and appear in the piece as in Example 6.[2]

Only in Variation I does a voice from the basic structure—the top voice, which is more sustained throughout—appear as a complete musical line (a "melody"). Otherwise the voices mix to form implied "polyphonic" lines, a technique familiar from compound melodies in Baroque music, especially Bach. Thus the sixteenth-note figure descending from the top voice's sustained B♭ at m. 1.1, D-A-C♯, contains the first notes of all three lower voices (and is therefore not itself directly derived from the underlying structure). Similarly, the four sixteenth notes at m. 13.1 (beginning Variation II), A♭-D♭-B♭-E♭, present the first notes of all four voices.

Each variation distributes the row in a different texture: Variation I is virtually homophonic in character, the sustained top voice set off against faster "accompanimental" figures; Variation II has a complex polyphonic texture; Variation III opens with—and continues to emphasize—a compound line that moves freely through all four voices of the underlying structure; and Variations IV and V return to a more contrapuntal texture.

The variations are also distinguished by "harmonic rhythm," determined by the number of beats within which the underlying structure is presented. Variation I, for example, comprises four appearances of the recurring three-measure metrical pattern underlying the piece, 3/4 + 2/4 + 3/4,[3] while the

---

2.   There is one exception: the order of the tenth and eleventh notes of the top voice of the third structure in Example 6, A-A♭, is reversed in the piece (m. 24). This may be a printing error, but it may also reflect a conscious decision made by the composer.

3.   This symmetrical three-measure grouping, 3 + 2 + 3 beats, mirrors the symmetry of the row structures.

other variations contain only two, thus doubling the harmonic density. Variation III doubles the values of the underlying pattern (3/2 + 2/2 + 3/2), however, and thus in effect returns to the lower rate of density.

The basic metrical unit is the quarter note, while the basic surface duration is the sixteenth, and much of the piece's rhythmic interest derives from the constant variation of the relationship between the sixteenth notes and the controlling beat. In the first half of Variation I (mm. 1–6), for example, all fifteen possible divisions of the quarter note by one to four sixteenth notes appear. (These measures contain a total of sixteen beats, the final quarter being a rest.)[4]

Another significant feature of the pitch structure concerns "harmony." Since the rows in Example 6 are purely linearly conceived, the four-part harmony produced by their simultaneous presentation is not directly derived from the series. As noted, however, the music does not project these chords as simultaneous events. Rather, the voices are distributed to form trichordal "verticalities" identical to the trichords found in the first hexachord (see Example 2). Thus the first three pitches in temporal proximity (m. 1), Bb-D-A, present a form of trichord i, while the next two groups of three, C#-Bb-A and Bb-A-F#, present forms of trichord iii. Throughout the composition the first note of each trichordal segmentation is set off by a change in articulation. (In the trichords just discussed, the first is articulated by a slur, the second by staccato, and the third by an accent.) In the first half of Variation I all four trichords appear "harmonically," whereas in each subsequent variation the vertical trichords are chosen to avoid duplication with the linear trichords generating the derived row(s) in that variation. For example, since the two derived rows in Variation II (rows C and A) are generated respectively by trichords i and iii, the harmonic trichords in this variation are limited to ii and iv; and since the single derived row in Variation III (row E) is generated by ii and iii, the harmonic trichords are limited to i and iv.

Further study of Example 6 reveals the extent to which the simultaneous rows of the five structures are interrelated. Each of the four voices in the first hexachord of Variations I and III is identical to the retrograde of one of the other voices in that hexachord (e.g., the first "soprano" hexachord is identical to the retrograde of the "tenor"), and in Variations II, IV, and V each voice in the first hexachord is identical to the second hexachord of one of the other voices (e.g., the soprano's first hexachord is identical to the alto's second). And in all five variations the entire second four-part hexachordal structure is a transposed retrograde of the first (mirroring the structure of the source row).

4.   This structural characteristic of the first six measures has led some analysts to view mm. 1–6 and 7–12 as separate units, designating them respectively as "Theme" and "Variation I" (as do both analyses cited in note 1). Other than textural similarity, the main rationale for considering mm. 1–12 as a single unit is that each of the five four-part structures in Example 6 corresponds to one formal unit.

24

GYÖRGY LIGETI (b. 1923)
Three Fantasies (1983), No. 2, *Wenn aus der Ferne*

⊗ Ah! = stets weich, ohne Akzent einsetzen.
⊗⊗ morendo: bocca chiusa.

Wenn aus der Ferne, da wir geschieden sind,	If out of the distance, since we are apart,
Ich dir noch kennbar bin, . . .	I am still recognizable to you, . . .
So sage, wie erwartet die Freundin dich?	Tell me, how does your friend await you?
In jenen Gärten, da nach entsetzlicher	In those gardens, where after terrible
Und dunkler Zeit wir uns gefunden?	And dark times we found each other?
. . . Wie flossen Stunden dahin, wie still	. . . How did the hours pass, how lifeless
War meine Seele über die Wahrheit daß	Was my soul at the truth that
Ich so getrennt gewesen wäre? . . .	I had been so alone? . . .
Wars Frühling? war es Sommer? die Nachtigall	Was it spring? was it summer? the nightingale
Mit süßem Liede lebte mit Völgen, die	With sweet song lived with birds that
Nicht ferne waren im Gebüsche	Were not far away in the shrubbery
Und mit Gerüchen umgaben Bäum' uns. . . .	And trees surrounded us with scents.
	. . .
Um Wänd und Mauern grünte der Epheu, grünt'	Around walls and fences the ivy grew, making green
Ein seelig Dunkel hoher Alleen. Offt	A soulful darkness of high alleys. Often
Des Abends, Morgens waren dort wir	In the evenings and mornings we were there
Redeten manches und sahn uns froh an.	Talking and looking at each other joyfully.
. . . Ach! wehe mir!	. . . Ah! woe is me!
Es waren schöne Tage. Aber	Those were beautiful days. But
Traurige Dämmerung folgte nachher.	Sad twilight followed.
Friedrich Hölderlin	Translated by Robert Morgan

ANALYTICAL COMMENTS

Ligeti's *Wenn aus der Ferne,* the second of three Hölderlin settings for mixed chorus (or, alternatively, chamber chorus, with one voice to a part), reflects a widespread tendency of the 1980s to reaffirm a more traditional compositional manner, while it simultaneously retains systematic procedures commonly found in music of the 1950s and 1960s. Thus the "micro-canonic" devices associated with Ligeti's development following *Atmosphères* (1961) still play a role, though applied in a less rigorous manner and in conjunction with clearly drawn melodic profiles and motives, resonant harmonies (at times with tonal suggestions), and a relatively traditional three-part form.

Hölderlin's poem, a complex evocation of memory and longing seen from the point of view of a woman looking back from the afterlife, dates from the poet's later years, when he was largely incapacitated by insanity, and was left incomplete at his death. Ligeti sets only those portions that supply the poem's basic narrative frame: (1) the woman considers the distance that separates her from her lover, (2) recalls their time of union (conveyed through idyllic images of a garden filled with birds, flowers, and greenery), and (3) despairs at the "sad twilight" that followed.

The setting conforms to this three-part textual structure giving rise to more chordally textured music; there are three sections, with each section further divided into two subsections. The overall formal and canonic layout is as follows:

TABLE 1

Section	Subsection	Canonic structure
I	*a* (mm. 1–17)	8-part / 4-part / 9-part
	b (mm. 19–27)	4-part
II	*a* (mm. 27–36)	9-part
	b (mm. 39–48)	4-part
III	*a* (mm. 49–53)	8-part
	b (mm. 55–68)	12-part

Each division is articulated by a break in canonic structure giving rise to more chordally textured music; otherwise the canons run essentially uninterrupted throughout. The noncanonic passages separating the two subsections in Sections I and III (mm. 17–18 and 53–55) are dynamically "neutral," punctuating the polyphony with more sustained music that provides a cadence of sorts (in both cases with significant overlapping). By contrast, the noncanonic passages separating Section I from Section II (mm. 26–27) and Section II from Section III (mm. 46–49), as well as the one separating the two subsections within Section II (mm. 33–36), provide climactic moments set off from their surroundings. Collectively, they form a three-phased climactic motion that reaches its apex at the end of Section II ("Ach! wehe mir!"). The sustained chord that closes the song, low in tessitura and dynamic level, completes a brief denouement provided by the final section, and is gradually filtered out from m. 65 on, the voices dropping off in descending order until the basses disappear into silence. Throughout, the chorus is divided into sixteen independent parts, producing dense webs of polyphonic sound.

The canonic structure varies, resisting simple description. The first subsection begins with an eight-part unison canon (female voices) that continues strictly in pitch and rhythm until m. 10 ("So sage"), where the voices reduce to four and the interval of imitation becomes a minor third. The nine-voice canon of the final phrase (m. 13, "In jenen Gärten") uses both a major second and a minor third as intervals of imitation. The lower, male voices "accompany" with more sustained lines that, while mimicking the canonic quality, are freely constructed, becoming increasingly active as the subsection nears its end.

The second subsection grows out of the lower voices held over after the "cadential" chord cuts off at m. 17.2. The altos begin with a four-part canon (m. 19), first at the unison, then major second (at m. 24.3). The lower voices, continuing noncanonically, again become more active near the end, contributing to the buildup toward the climax that terminates Section I.

Section II is clearly set off texturally, by solo voices (if full chorus is used), male as well as female canonic voices, higher tessitura, and the absence of sustained lower voices. A nine-part canon continues throughout most of the first subsection (mm. 27–33), the interval of imitation only regularized (at a major third) after the opening words "die Nachtigall." Minor rhythmic alterations introduced in mm. 31.4–33.1 bring the voices closer together as they build toward the more massive, noncanonic texture at mm. 33–36. (The only noncanonic material preceding this is the basses' brief echo of "war's Sommer?," mm. 27.6–28, and their "Um Wänd' und Mauern," mm. 31.5–32.) All voices participate in the noncanonic climax ending this subsection. In the second subsection, more sustained, noncanonic music returns in the lower voices (now including the alto), while the sopranos have a four-part unison canon, again interrupted for the climactic tutti (mm. 46–47).

The eight-part unison canon in the alto and tenor voices that opens Section III is interrupted in mm. 53–55.3, articulating the end of the first subsection, after which a twelve-part unison canon opens the final subsection. As the last notes of this canon sustain, the sopranos bring back the opening phrase of the text (m. 57.3). A series of attacks activating the closing chord, notably in the basses in mm. 64–67, offer a final, weak echo of the canonic processes underlying the work.

The canonic upper voices are primarily responsible for the musical continuity, presenting most of the text in sequential order; while the more sustained, noncanonic lower voices have a more accompanimental role, presenting textual fragments out of order. Significantly, the only three portions of text not set canonically ("War's Frühling? war es Sommer?"; "Um Wänd und Mauern grünte der Epheu, grünt' ein seelig Dunkel hoher Alleen"; and "Ach! wehe mir!") appear at the three climactic moments.

Despite the "learned" canonic character, traditional features abound. The imitative relationships are usually perceptible (differentiating them from those in such earlier Ligeti compositions as *Lontano*), and the individual canonic voices mirror the rhythmic and syntactic structure of the text closely, just as the overall form mirrors its semantic divisions.

Although the harmonic language is densely chromatic, there is sufficient emphasis on thirds so that the vertical structures have definite triadic resonances. The opening melodic figure outlines a C♯-minor chord, while the more slowly moving lower voices arpeggiate the C♯-E third of that triad, after opening on a mildly dissonant A (a note also associated melodically with C♯ and G♯ in mm. 4–7). The lower voices close on a different fifth,

B♭–F (m. 8.5), confirming the melodic F that closes the first phrase of the canon, supplying a kind of cadence, and also supporting the canonic entrances on B♭ that initiate the second phrase. In general, the melodic lines are diatonically conceived; they are associated with imitations at the unison, major second, and major and minor thirds, and produce less harmonic density than the more cluster-dominated canons in Ligeti's earlier compositions.

Another traditional feature is found in recurring motives in the canonic lines. These are repeated both immediately, in consequence of canonic imitation, and over larger spans. The most important is the opening C♯ triadic figure, which reappears with the same rhythm and contour (though closing with a third rather than fifth) at the beginning of the second subsection of Section I. It also reappears in Section III, where it opens both subsections, at m. 49 (in a slightly accelerated form, and with a closing sixth) and m. 55 (with a falling contour, heard previously in the second phrase of the first section, mm. 7–8). Finally, this motive appears in an augmented rhythm (again with a rising sixth) in conjunction with the return of the opening line of the text in mm. 57–58.

Though the contrasting middle section begins with a different motive (m. 27.4), it continues with an accelerated version of the triadic figure (mm. 28–30). An additional motivic recurrence connects the two climactic points of this section; the top voice of the second (mm. 46–48) presents a reordered version of the top voice of the first (mm. 33–36), the four highest pitches being identical.

25

KARLHEINZ STOCKHAUSEN (b. 1928)
Kreuzspiel (1951), first movement

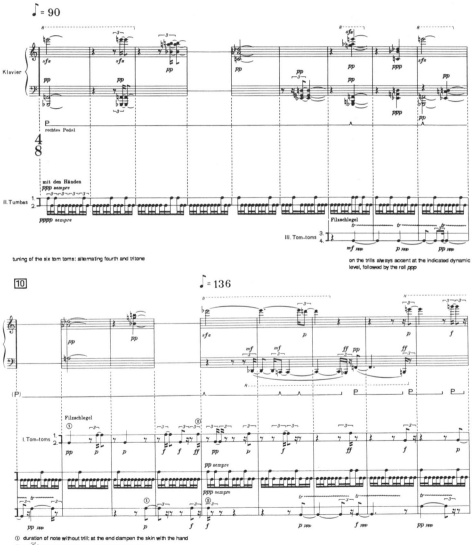

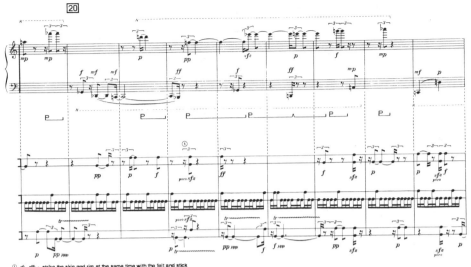

① *sfz, sffz* = strike the skin and rim at the same time with the felt and stick

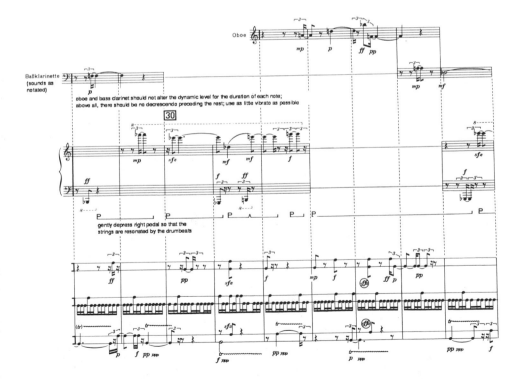

oboe and bass clarinet should not alter the dynamic level for the duration of each note;
above all, there should be no decrescendo preceding the rest; use as little vibrato as possible

gently depress right pedal so that the
strings are resonated by the drumbeats

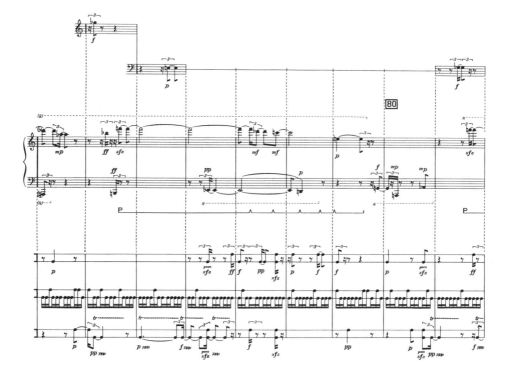

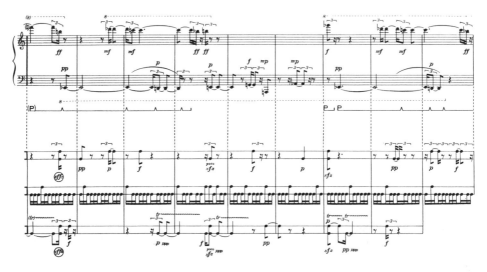

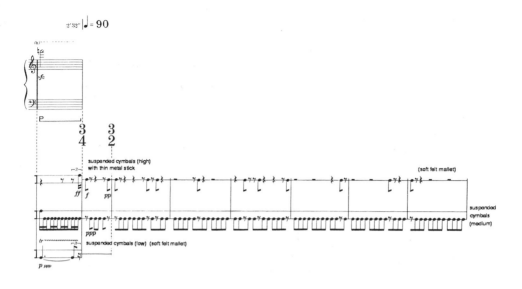

ANALYTICAL COMMENTS

Kreuzspiel, one of the definitive works of integral serialism, was Stockhausen's first composition in this manner. The piece is consistent with the "pointillistic" approach favored by many younger Europeans of the time, in which numerical series are applied to various parameters of the music, including pitch, rhythm, and register, each unfolding essentially independently of the others.

Even at this early stage, however, one recognizes Stockhausen's tendency to shape music through large dramatic gestures. Thus the first of *Kreuzspiel*'s three movements (played without pause) follows a simple underlying plan whose general outline can easily be followed by the listener, lending coherence to the individual serial operations.

Kreuzspiel means 'cross play" or "crisscross," an idea reflected both in the details of the serial manipulations and in the movement's overall plan. The latter involves a gradual exchange of the two hexachords of the original pitch series over the course of the movement; one moves upward, one pitch at a time, from the lowest register to the highest, while the other moves downward, from the highest to the lowest, the two "crossing" in the middle. Following a brief introduction, the piano states the pitch series linearly (mm. 14–20.2), the first hexachord placed in the extreme upper register (right hand) and the second in the extreme lower (left hand). During the movement the right-hand pitches move downward and the left-hand pitches move upward, so that at the end the hexachords are reversed: the first hexachord is in the lowest register, the second in the highest. As they change register, the pitches pass from piano to woodwinds as they enter the middle registers, then pass back again to the piano as they approach the opposite extreme. A clear timbral-registral transformation results, shaped so that it ends as it began, but with hexachords reversed.

The original pitch series undergoes a complex twelve-stage rotation (see Example 1),[1] designed so that the final rotation produces the hexachordal reversal required by the overall plan. The second half of this twelve-stage structure is a mirror of the first half. Another significant feature is that pairs of pitches symmetrically placed with reference to the hexachordal division (those in order positions 1 and 12, 2 and 11, 3 and 10, etc.) remain symmetrically placed throughout, though their position and hexachordal membership varies.

EXAMPLE 1

The durations of these pitches are determined by numbers assigned to each pitch, indicating their length measured in triplet sixteenth notes (the

1.   Example 1 and Tables 1 and 2 are similar to Examples 1 and 2 in Jonathan Harvey's *The Music of Stockhausen* (Berkeley and Los Angeles, 1975), pp. 18 and 20. (The book provides an excellent introduction to Stockhausen's work through the 1960s.)

basic rhythmic unit of the movement). The numbers chosen for the original row are then subjected to the same rotations as the pitches:

TABLE 1

I	11	5	6	9	2	12	|	1	10	4	7	8	3
II	5	6	9	2	12	3	|	11	1	10	4	7	8
III	6	9	2	12	8	11	|	3	5	1	10	4	7

etc.

Each row totals seventy-eight triplet sixteenths, or six and a half bars of 4/8 meter, so that the twelve rotations divide the main body of the movement into twelve equal segments: I (mm. 14–20.2), II (20.3–26), III (27–33.2), IV (33.3–39), V (40–46.2), VI (46.3–52), VII (53–59.2), VIII (59.3–65), IX (66–72.2), X (72.3–78), XI (79–85.2), and XII (85.3–91).

Since the pitch and duration series are rotated identically, each pitch is consistently linked with the same duration (all E♭'s with eleven triplet sixteenths, all D♭'s with five triplet sixteenths, etc.). These durations are measured by the distance between successive attacks, however, not by the length of the pitch itself. For example, although there are eleven triplet sixteenths between the right-hand E♭ in m. 14 and the left-hand D♭ that follows, as required by the series, the E♭ is actually longer (sustained until the right hand's next pitch); and although there are ten triplet sixteenths between the right-hand E at m. 17.4 and the right-hand G at 18.3, as required, the E lasts only eight triplet sixteenths.

The instrumental distribution within the twelve sections is tied to the overall registral conception. In the first, second, and final sections, all notes are played by the piano. As the pitches migrate toward the middle registers, the woodwinds start playing them, increasing from two pitches in Section III to six in Sections IV and V, to ten in Section VI. This last section, the midpoint of the movement, has the greatest number of middle register (woodwind) pitches, only one pitch remaining in the piano's highest and one in its lowest register. The woodwinds then decrease as the pitches move toward the opposite registral extremes, from seven in Section VII to five in VIII, four in IX, two in X, and one in XI.

The specific registers are determined by an additional numerical series: 7-2-5-4-3-6-1, with 7 representing the lowest octave of the piano—A^0 through $G\#^1$—and 1 representing the highest, A^6 through $G\#^7$ (the four highest piano notes, A^7-C^8, are not used). Each pitch follows this series, those originally in the left hand (second hexachord) progressing from left to right (7, 2, 5, etc.), those in the right hand (first hexachord) moving from right to left (1, 6, 3, etc.). Since the extreme registers (7 and 1) are placed at the edges of the series, followed by 2 and 6, 5 and 3, and 4 (the middle register) in the middle, this generates the previously discussed registral crisscross; the six pitches originally in the lowest octave (7) end in the highest (1), and vice versa.

Running concurrently with the linked pitch and rhythmic structures of Example 1 and Table 1 are two purely rhythmic structures, one played by four tom-toms (two percussionists playing two drums each) and the other by two tumbas (a finger drum). After opening with an introductory series of regularly decreasing durations, from twelve triplet sixteenths to one (mm. 7.3–13), the tom-toms begin a series at m. 14 that is rotated exactly like the durational series of Table 1:

TABLE 2

I	2	8	7	4	11	1		12	3	9	6	5	10
II	8	7	4	11	1	10		2	12	3	9	6	5
III	7	4	11	1	5	2		10	8	12	3	9	6

etc.

The distribution of durations among the four tom-toms is also determined: the first drum is always given durations 1, 4, and 7, the second 3, 6, and 8, the third 2, 5, and 9, and the fourth 10, 11, and 12. Occasional additional attacks are inserted (twenty-four in all), distinguishable from the others by being played *sforzando* by two or more drums simultaneously. These additions are always short (without roll), and always coincide with a pitch attack.

The tumbas project the basic unit of measure, playing constant triplet sixteenths throughout and articulating each duration with an attack on the smaller (higher) drum. They begin (mm. 1–7.2) by introducing the series that will initiate the tom-toms' rotation at m. 14 (2, 8, 7, 11, etc.). Instead of rotating this series, however, they continue with a series that increases regularly from a single triplet sixteenth to twelve, retrograding the simultaneously decreasing series in the tom-toms (another crisscross). Unlike all the other components, which begin rotational structures at m. 14, the tumbas begin their rotational process at m. 7.3 with this increasing series. Though similar to the others, the rotation is somewhat simpler:

TABLE 3

I	1	2	3	4	5	6		7	8	9	10	11	12
II	2	3	4	5	6	12		1	7	8	9	10	11
III	3	4	5	6	12	11		2	1	7	8	9	10

etc.

The seventh rotation produces an exact retrograde of the original series (1, 2, 3, . . . becomes 12, 11, 10, . . .). This easily recognizable accelerating row occurs simultaneously with the sixth row of the pitch structure, accompanying the midpoint of the movement's registral transformations (mm. 46.3–52, all but two pitches played by woodwinds), a moment dramatized by the substitution of woodblock for small tumba to announce the durational beginnings. The final six rotations bring the tumba series back to its original (increasing) form, which coincides with the final pitch series and thus similarly articulates the return of all pitches to the piano (mm. 85.3–91).

Despite the care with which the systematic aspects of the composition have been worked out, the various serial structures are not absolutely strictly adhered to in the compositional realization. Typically for Stockhausen's serial music, there are a few alterations (for example, the order of two pitches or durations is reversed), though these are very much the exception in this piece. Moreover, even when there are changes (as, notably, in the pitched instruments of mm. 59.3–65), each segment invariably contains the requisite twelve pitches and seventy-eight triplet sixteenths.

The purely percussive passage beginning at m. 92 signals the end of the movement, its transitional function reflected in the first appearance of a cymbal. The second movement (not included here) presents a registral "inversion" of the first, with pitches beginning in the middle register and moving outward, while the final movement combines the motions of the previous two, producing a texture of considerably greater density.

26

GEORGE CRUMB (b. 1929)
Night of the Four Moons (1969), No. 1, *La luna está muerta, muerta . . .*

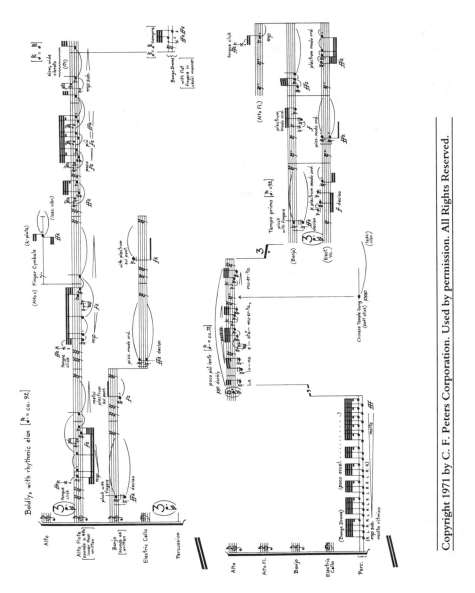

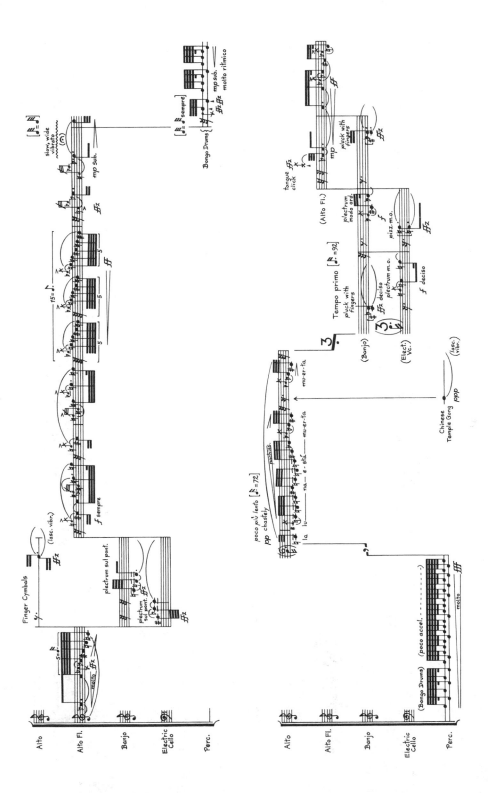

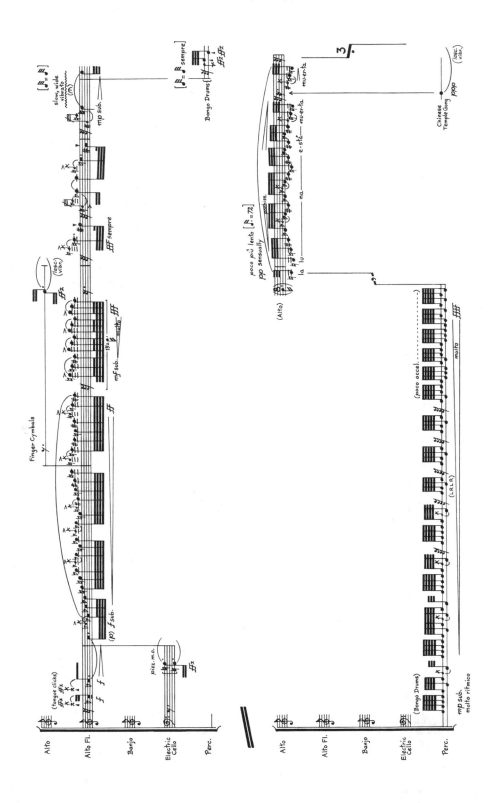

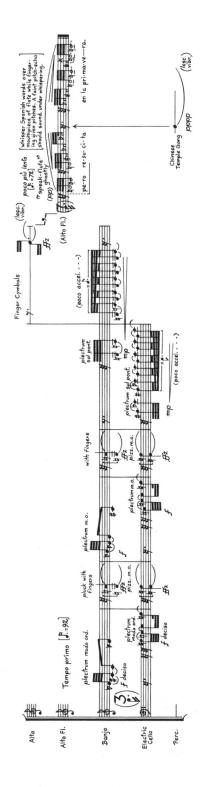

La luna está muerta, muerta . . .
pero resucita en la primavera.

Federico García Lorca

The moon is dead, dead . . . .
but it is reborn in the springtime.

Translated by J. L. Gili. From *Selected Poems by Federico García Lorca*. Copyright 1955 by New Directions Publications. Used by permission of New Directions Publications.

ANALYTICAL COMMENTS

This song, the first of four, was composed during the Apollo 11 flight, the first manned voyage to the moon. Crumb has said of *Night of the Four Moons:* "I suppose . . . [it] is really an 'occasional' work, since its inception was an artistic response to an external event. The texts—extracts from the poems of Federico García Lorca—symbolize my own rather ambivalent feelings *vis-à-vis* Apollo 11."[1]

"La luna está muerta, muerta . . ." (The moon is dead, dead . . .) reflects this ambivalence. Its highly colorful, quasi-primitive style, evocative of non-Western folk and ethnic traditions, represents a type much in vogue during the 1960s and 1970s. Exotic timbres produced by a banjo, an "electric cello" (cello amplified through a contact microphone), finger cymbals, a Chinese temple gong, and bongos, along with the more breathy, low-pitched alto flute (rather than the normal C flute), evoke an aura of mystery and elusiveness. In addition, unusual performance techniques de-familiarize the sounds: the banjo and cello play pizzicato throughout, often using a plectrum to produce harsh, percussive attacks, while the flutist employs tongue clicks, decorative grace notes, and on occasion a slow, wide vibrato. Nonmetrical rhythmic patterns with "additive" durations and highly ornamented, repetitious chantlike melodies contribute to the otherworldly musical atmosphere.

A primitive flavor derives from the monophonic texture—despite alternations of instruments and colors, only one event occurs at a time—and from the highly formalized, almost ritualistic, ceremonial quality of the musical gestures. This ceremonial quality is especially evident in the percussively conceived instrumental parts, which seem to summon the more melodic alto flute and voice with short, annunciatory signals. The piece almost sounds like an attempt to reconstruct a lost aboriginal music, native to some entirely different realm (perhaps the moon itself?).

Adding to this quality is the highly formalized structure: a simple four-part strophic setting, with each strophe subdivided into a series of four fixed formal units. The sequence of units is as follows: (1) a plucked banjo–cello "introduction," interwoven with short flute interjections (which are always preceded by tongue clicks) and terminating with a sustained attack on finger cymbals; (2) an alto flute solo (without an initiating tongue click), leading to a sustained note played with a slow vibrato; (3) a rhythmically differentiated "roll" on bongos, with a crescendo and final accelerando, providing an annunciatory upbeat to (4) a vocal setting of a single line of text, punctuated by a soft, low gong stroke.

Although this sequence remains largely in place in each strophe, significant alterations confer upon the music a more encompassing shape and lend it a quasi-improvisational quality. During the first three strophes the content of three of the four subunits is progressively expanded (the exception

1.   Quoted from the liner notes of the 1974 recording on Columbia Records, M 32739.

is the introduction, which contracts and expands in a symmetrical pattern, 18-16-16-18 dotted-sixteenth units); and the flute moves higher in each lengthening segment. This process reaches a climactic point in the third strophe, which is also set apart by the delay of the finger cymbal punctuation (which had ended the introduction in the previous strophes) until the flute has crested.

The most striking alterations, however, come in the final strophe, in conjunction with the long-delayed setting of the poem's second line (the first three strophes simply repeated the first line). Although the introduction regains its original (longer) duration, the other units are considerably shortened, with the flute and voice now united in a single, transfiguring event: the final line is whispered over the instrument's mouthpiece as pitches are simultaneously fingered, creating a disembodied "flute-voice," a ghostly presence evoking the rebirth promised in the text. The voice part itself is entirely absent from the strophe, as are the flute's introductory interjections and the bongo's ominous roll. (The bongo roll, which would have overwhelmed the delicate aura of the final line, is faintly mirrored in the final tremolos of the banjo and cello). Everything is simplified, focusing attention upon the final epiphany.

The pitch structure, modal in conception and severely limited in content, supports the air of archaic simplicity. The basic scalar unit is a gapped symmetrical whole-tone segment (0,2,6,8), one transposition of which—G^3-A^3-$C\sharp^4$-$E\flat^4$—controls the banjo-cello music throughout (with one exception, mentioned below). The voice uses the same four pitches, plus a non-whole-tone $G\flat^4$, always treated as a grace note. The pitch basis for the alto flute part, outlined in Example 1 (transposed to concert pitch), is slightly more complex.

The bar lines in the example separate the content of the four strophes (indicated by Roman numerals), while the dotted bar lines indicate segmentations within the strophes. The same four-pitch whole-tone cell underlies this music as well, and is placed in boxes in the example. (Pitch groups in boxes with dotted lines contain only three of the four pitches in this cell.) Unlike the voice and banjo-flute components, the flute transposes the cell in the second and third strophes, shifting from one of the two possible whole-tone scales to the other and back again.

EXAMPLE 1

In the first segment of the flute's second strophe, a non–whole-tone $G\flat^4$ is added, mirroring the alto voice's $G\flat^4$ in the first strophe. The $G\flat^4$ initially appears as a grace note (again mirroring the voice), but later becomes the lowest pitch of the transposition in the flute's second segment. During that segment, and again in the third strophe, the $E\flat^4$ of the previous cell is retained so that minor thirds appear on both sides of the basic unit, creating a more expanded symmetrical structure. In the "introduction" to the final strophe, this expanded unit is transferred to the banjo and cello, no doubt to represent the missing flute, when $G\flat^4$ and E^3 are added to their basic four-note repertory.

The only element of the alto flute part not directly derived from the scalar structures of Example 1 are the minor-ninth figures heard at the end of the first three strophes (the longer notes elaborated by these figures maintain the underlying whole-tone relationships). These ninths are prepared by the major-seventh boundaries resulting from the addition of non–whole-tone pitches a minor third above the basic cell, that is, the boundary from G^3 to $G\flat^4$ in the voice and flute parts.

27

KRZYSZTOF PENDERECKI (b. 1933)
Threnody for the Victims of Hiroshima (1960)

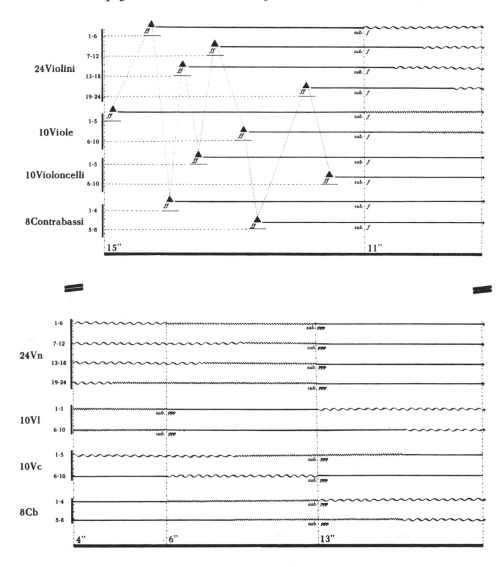

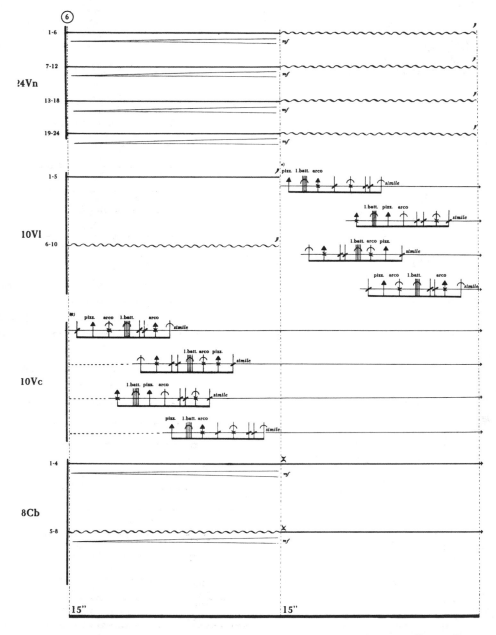

Each instrumentalist chooses one of the 4 given groups and executes it (within a fixed space of time) as rapidly as possible.

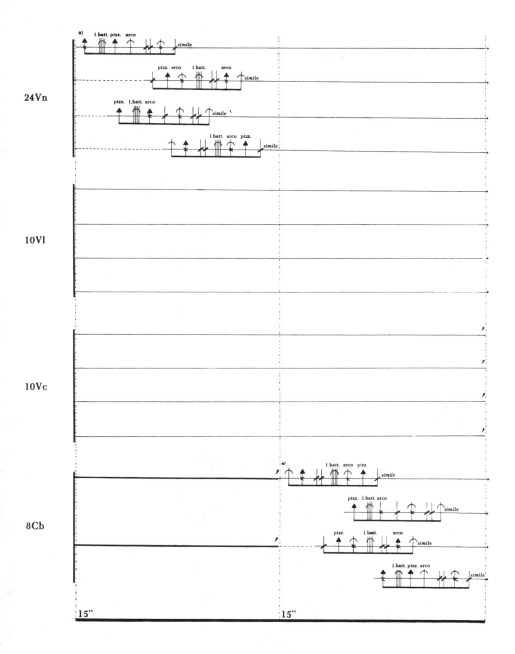

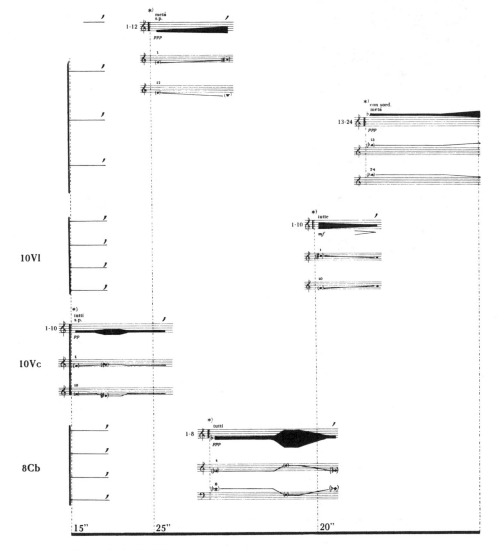

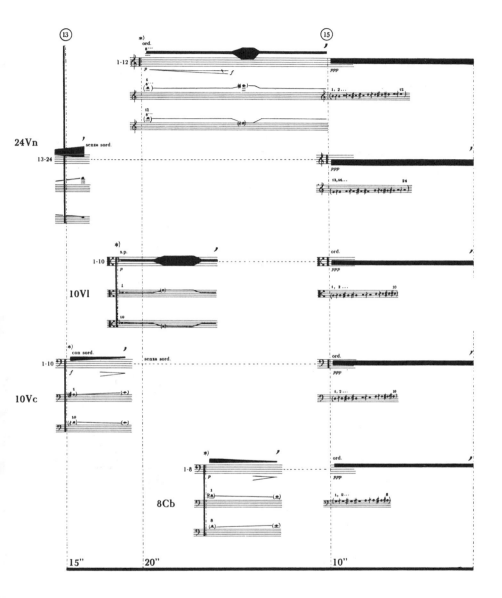

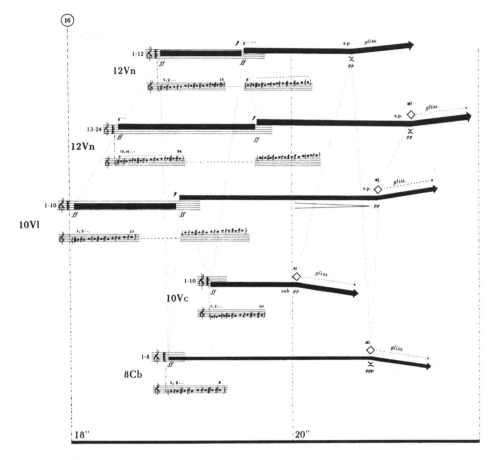

*) flageolet tones

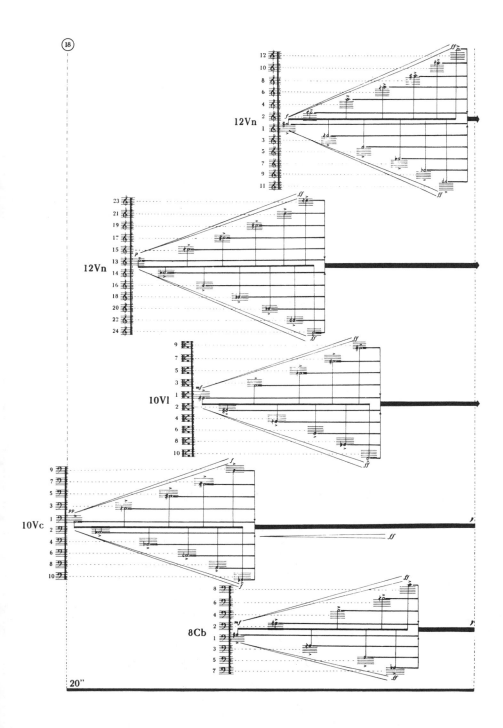

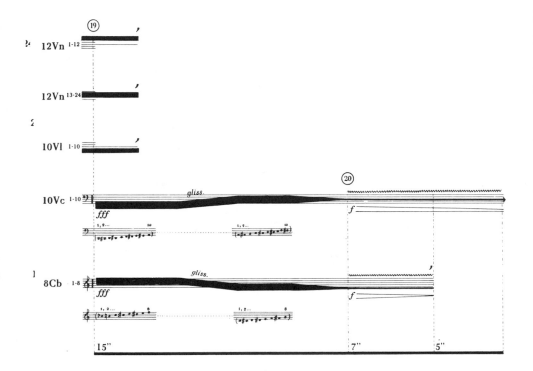

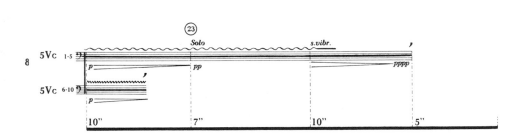

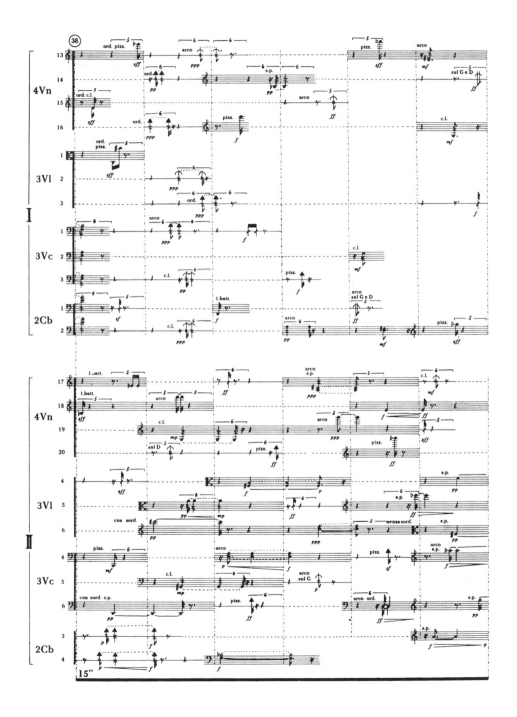

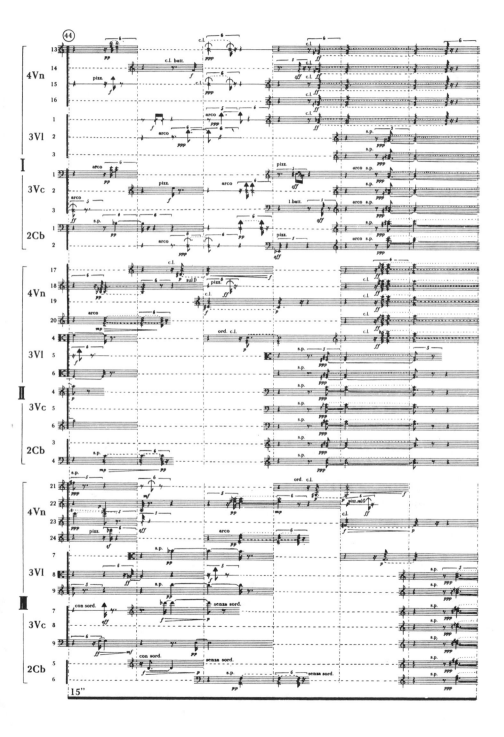

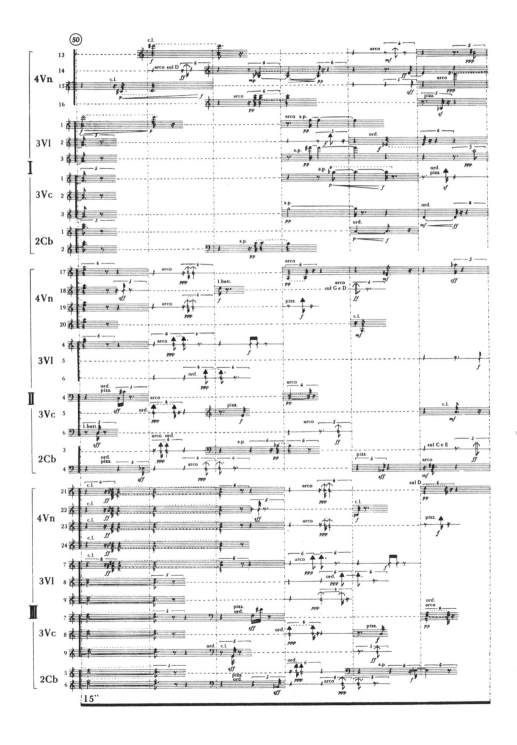

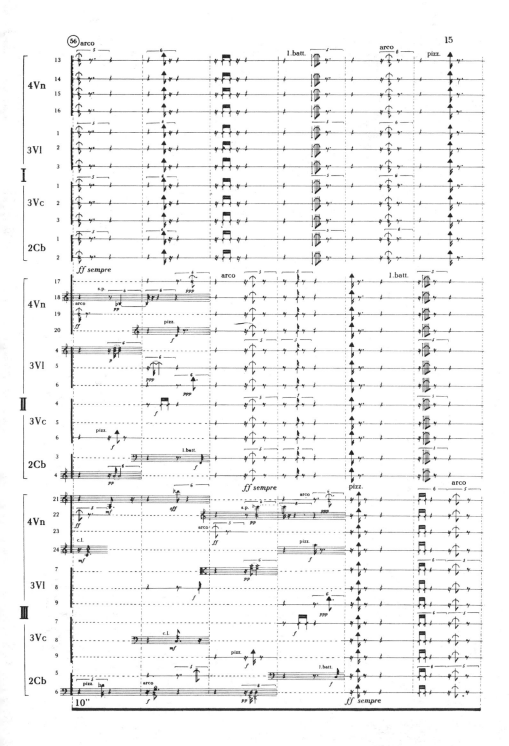

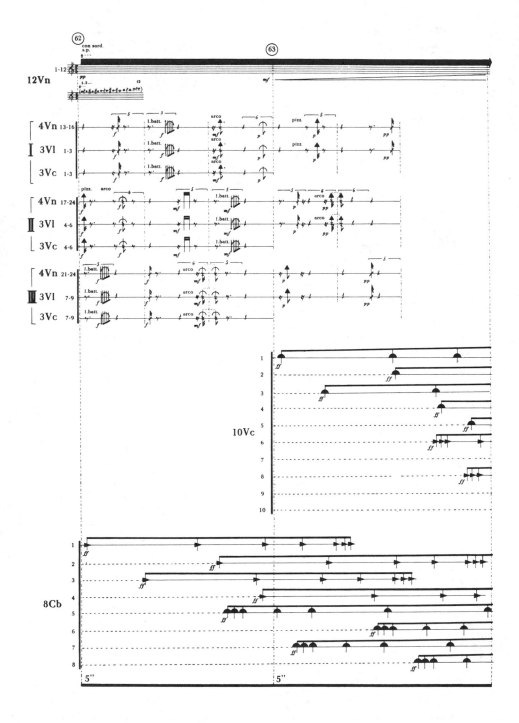

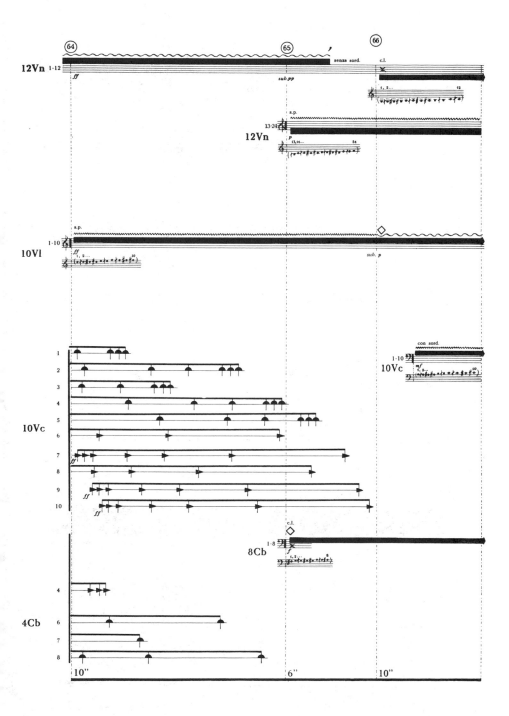

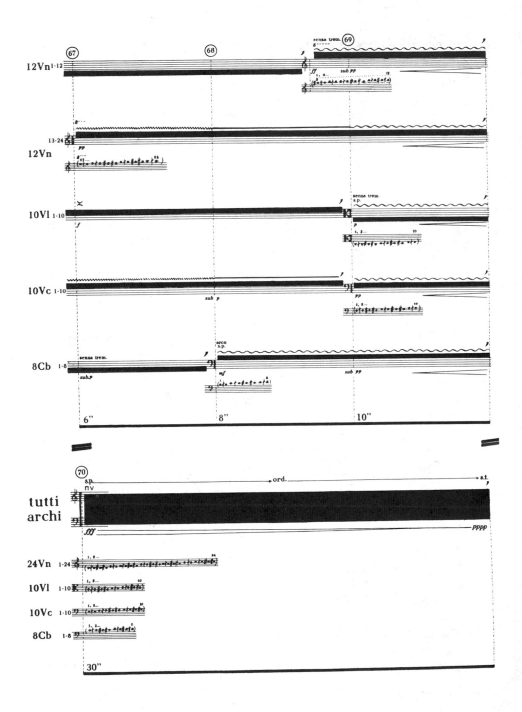

**ABBREVIATIONS
AND SYMBOLS**

ord.
s. p.
s. t.
c. l.
l. batt.

raised by ¼ tone	⊬
raised by ¾ tone	⧣
lowered by ¼ tone	ↆ
lowered by ¾ tone	ⅾ
highest note of the in- strument (indefinite pitch)	▲
play between bridge and tailpiece	↑
arpeggio on 4 strings behind the bridge	⧻
play on tailpiece (arco)	⊢
play on bridge	♟
percussion effect: strike the upper sounding board of the violin with the nut or the finger-tips	♪
several irregular changes of bow	⊓ V
molto vibrato	∿
very slow vibrato with a ¼ tone frequency differ- ence produced by slid- ing the finger	∿∿
very rapid not rhythmi- cized tremolo	ⳤ

ANALYTICAL COMMENTS

Penderecki's *Threnody* was an extremely influential composition during the 1960s, when it helped define a widespread tendency toward "textural composition." In this music, even more than in integral serialism, traditional textural components such as melody and harmony are absent. Even well-defined individual pitches and rhythmic patterns are missing throughout much of the work. Emphasis is on bands of sounds, or clusters, treated as composite units, and on the overall textural effect. Form is thus primarily determined by the transformation and development of generalized shapes.

The string ensemble is not organized according to the normal five-part grouping; each instrument has its own independent part, permitting extremely dense textures. Groups of instruments are nevertheless often notated as single events, especially in producing bands of closely spaced pitches; for example, at m. 15 five quarter-tone bands fill in most of the space between G^2 and F^5 (the precise pitches of each part indicated beneath the notated bands), while at m. 10 ten cellos start together on F^4 and expand outward until they fill in the perfect fourth $D\sharp^4$-$G\sharp^4$.

Since the rhythmic structure is not metrical, traditional rhythmic notation is largely replaced by "spatial" notation, featuring rhythmic units (indicated by dotted vertical lines) of variable lengths measured in seconds (the first lasting fifteen seconds, the second lasting eleven, etc.). The temporal placement of musical events is only approximate, indicated by the relative spatial position within these rhythmic units. Much of *Threnody* also makes use of nonconventional playing techniques, which are listed (along with their notational symbols) on a page following the score.

Despite all that is new in this music, a number of traditional features are recognizable, especially in the larger organization. The work divides clearly into three parts, the second providing a contrasting middle section, the third returning to music that resembles the opening. The division between the first two sections is unambiguous: the middle section begins with an abrupt change of texture and timbre (m. 26), preceded by a long, sustained single note with diminuendo leading to five seconds of silence. The second and third sections overlap, the third beginning some eight seconds before the second ends (mm. 63–64). We shall see that several additional factors link these sections.

The first section of *Threnody* is divided into three subsections. It opens with a series of "imitative" entrances, with ten groups of instruments entering with their "highest" (indefinite) pitch. By the end of the first fifteen-second "measure" (the term is retained here, though its meaning must be adjusted), a band of very loud, high ("screeching") sound has accumulated; and the remainder of the first subsection involves the gradual transformation of this sound. It becomes suddenly less loud at m. 2, and gradually begins to waver as one by one the instrument groups add vibrato. The activation of the sound is carried a step further at m. 6, when the instrument groups start playing successions of seven short, separately attacked sounds in altering sequences. Although the effect sounds random, each group plays one of four closely corresponding seven-event sequences (one of the four, for example, is the retrograde of another). These short sounds are also brought in one by one, in quasi-imitative fashion, gradually infiltrating the sustained sound of the opening, which has completely disappeared by the end of m. 9. By then, the short events create what sounds like a beehive of activity, producing an effect still similar to an unbroken band of sound, but one that has become internally activated.

The completion of this transformational process marks the close of the first subsection. The second subsection begins at m. 10 with an abrupt return to the less active, sustained quality of the opening, now in a lower register. Once again the texture develops through quasi-imitative entrances, in this case involving clusters that expand and contract in glissando-like motions. The subsection ends in m. 16 with a dissolution process, as the various strands glide off in different directions, again one by one, eventually falling into silence. The final subsection (m. 18) features a series of outward expansions from single pitches (recalling the previous segment's glissando expansions), again in imitation, this time building to a thick, climactic cluster by m. 19, after which another dissolution sets in with glissandos, gradually filtering out until only a single cello remains (m. 23).

The middle section's "pointillistic" texture sets it off sharply from the previous music. Here durations are traditionally notated, but the complex rhythmic relationships assure that no definite metrical pattern emerges (varying quintuplet and sextuplet subdivisions are especially prominent). Most of the middle section is constructed as a strict three-part canon (though with several "mistakes"), with the strings divided into three "orchestras," one for each part (indicated by Roman numerals on the left side of the score). Table 1 outlines the relationships of the three canonic parts.

TABLE 1

mm. 26   30   35   40   45
                                                    ← →
I: 1 2 3 4 5 6 7 8 9 10 11 12 13 14 15 16 17 17 16 15 14

                                II: 1   2   3   4   5   6   7   8   9

                                            III: 5   6   7

mm.   50   55   60

I: | 13 12 11 10 | 9 8 7 6 5 X X X X X X X X
                              ← →
II: | 10 11 12 13 | 14 15 16 17 17 16 15 X X X X X X
                                    ← →
III: 8 9 | 10 11 12 13 | 14 15 16 17 17 16 15 X X X X

The numbers in the body of the table refer to content relationships among the three orchestras, not actual measures—all 1's contain canonically related material, as do all 2's, and so on. Orchestra I opens the section (m. 26), Orchestra II begins twelve measures later (m. 38), and Orchestra III begins six measures after that (m. 44). Since mm. 1–4 are omitted in Orchestra III, a two-measure temporal interval separates it from Orchestra II (m. 44 in III corresponding to m. 42 in II, etc.). In addition, all three orchestras begin retrograding after their seventeenth measure.

Orchestra II imitates Orchestra I at the original pitch, but with instruments and registers reversed: the bass Bb^1 on the downbeat of m. 26, for example, becomes the violin Bb^3 on the downbeat of m. 36, the violin harmonic F^7 on the downbeat of m. 28 becomes the bass harmonic F^4 on the downbeat of m. 40, and so on. Orchestra III imitates Orchestra II transposed either up a fourth or down a fifth, also with instruments and registers reversed. All three retrogrades are at the original pitch, again with reversed instruments and registers.

Although the complexity of both the individual "voices" and the canonic relationships connecting them renders this canon imperceptible, it produces a textural accumulation analogous to the relationships formed by the imitative processes of the first section. In addition, the canonic and retrograde structures are arranged so that the sustained chords in Orchestra I at mm. 35–38 (10–13 in Table 1), which stand out from the otherwise fragmented texture, appear in all three orchestras in mm. 47–52 (boxed in the table).

Their coincidence marks the first phase of a process of mediation between the predominantly pointillistic texture of the middle section and the more sustained texture of the final section. The second phase begins where the strict retrograde and canonic structures break off—m. 56 in Orchestra I, m. 58 in II, and m. 60 in III—as the three orchestras present in free imitation, at two-measure intervals, short yet coordinated ensemble attacks (indicated with X's in the table), employing performance techniques introduced at m. 6 of the first section.

The final phase begins with the high violin cluster and imitative bass and cello entrances at m. 62, which bring back the more sustained texture of the opening section, overlapping with the continuing short sounds of the middle section. The third section forms an essentially unbroken gesture, building toward a final climactic cluster that bursts in triple *forte* at m. 70, mirroring the climactic development of the third subsection of the first part. This cluster is sustained for thirty seconds while the dynamic level decreases, and the piece concludes by fading into silence, in a manner again recalling the close of the first section.

28

PETER MAXWELL DAVIES (b. 1934)
Vesalii icones (1969), Nos. 1, 6, 8, and 14

1. Agony in the Garden

*) The letters in the Autoharp line refer to the glossary.

*) The small notes represent alternatives for the Clarinet in A.

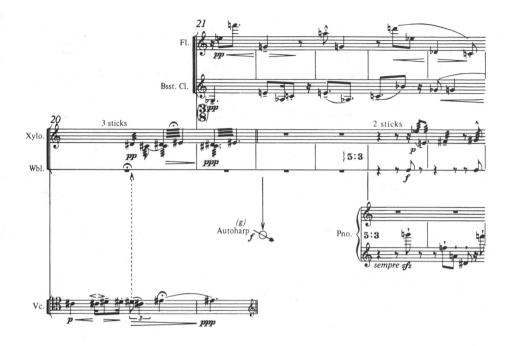

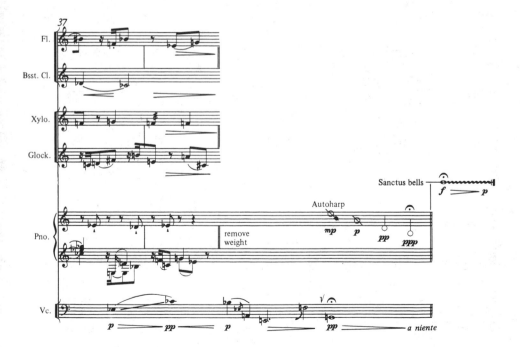

6. The Mocking of Christ

*) Each player has 3 or 4 'groups'. He plays these in various orders, freely, starting quietly and slowly and increasing speed and loudness. Order of entry is given. (1st, 2nd, 3rd, 4th). When dancer plays his piano, each player completes his 'group' – *dim e rit.* The honky-tonk starts when the above instrumental figures are well established; as soon as the honky-tonk is heard, the conductor cuts the other instruments.

) Instrumentalists enter **pp *adagio* with their 'groups' as before, *accel/cresc.* as before. Xylophone in addition, enters after Dancer's piano has stopped. Instrumentalists stop as before on Dancer's second piano entry.

8. St. Veronica wipes His Face

*) The pianist records bars 259-262 (as far as the downbeat) on a cheap commercial tape recorder, (during performance with cellist).

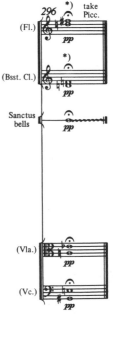

The pianist starts music-box at
3rd measure of tape-recording
and fades tape at Conductor's
direction.

Musicians imitate quietly motifs
of music box, Vla. and Vc. *pizz.*
Percussion has glockenspiel.

Pianist stops music box at
Conductor's direction. Fade out;
pause.

start playback of tape-recording

*) Hum one note, play the other, (the hummed one may be in another octave).

14. Resurrection - Antichrist

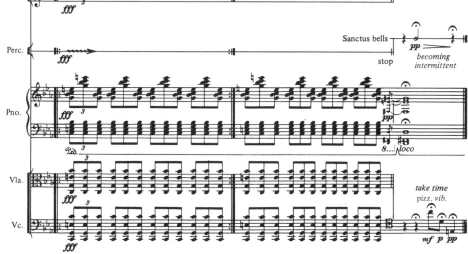

Glossary of out-of-tune Autoharp symbols
The letters refer to specific symbols used in the score

(a)   Across the strings freely with the stick. The pitches in the autoharp part are approximately indicated only.

(b)   A single stroke on a deep resonant string.

(c)   Strike the wood of the instrument with the stick (wooden end); the strings vibrate sympathetically.

(d)   A deep gong sound — low strings.

(e)   The stick is drawn quickly across all the strings, up and down.

(f)   The stick (wooden end), or a finger-nail, is drawn down a single string; choose a covered string.

(g)   A single stroke downwards across all strings.

ANALYTICAL COMMENTS

Vesalii icones, a set of fourteen dances, is one of several theatrical chamber pieces incorporating religious elements that Davies composed during the later 1960s. Scored for solo cello, dancer, and small ensemble (flute, clarinet, viola, percussion, and piano), the work relies upon quotation and parody to project multiple, intertwined levels of musical and dramatic meaning.

Each dance is associated with one of the drawings from *De humani corporis fabrica,* a book of anatomical studies by Andreas Vesalius dating from the sixteenth century, and each is associated as well with one of the fourteen stations of the cross from the Passion of Christ. The dancer begins with the body position given in the drawing and moves to depict symbolically the Passion scene. Davies refers to a "three-tiered set of [dramatic] superpositions":[1] the Vesalius illustrations, the stations of the cross, and the dancer's own body. And there are three corresponding musical superpositions: popular music, Renaissance polyphony, and his own music. But as we shall see, it is difficult to keep the musical styles distinct.

The four dances included here, taken from the opening, central, and closing portions of the work, provide an overview of the musical and dramatic character. Quotation and parody abound, ranging from banal popular music to Renaissance sacred polyphony, suggesting that nothing is necessarily what it seems to be and that any one thing can turn into another, including its apparent opposite. The eclectic compositional mix even includes procedures reminiscent of serialism, though in a non-twelve-tone context and adapted to a manner quite distant from the rarified style with which they are normally associated.

No. 1, "Agony in the Garden," opens with an extended solo cello line, accompanied by percussive commentary on the autoharp and sustained notes in the winds (mostly doublings of cello pitches). In the first of a series of

---

1.   This and subsequent quotations are from the composer's liner notes for the 1974 recording, Nonesuch H-71295.

declamatory gestures closing with fermatas, the cello presents a five-note sequence that contains all but one note of a whole-tone scale, then continues (m. 2) with an inversion of the gesture, introducing the missing whole-tone pitch (D). Afterward the cello line develops more freely, continuing to emphasize whole-tone relations.

At m. 8 three brief canons begin, based on the previous cello music. The flute takes its pitches directly from the cello part, which it divides into three segments, one for each canon. The other voices transpose and retrograde the flute part, and in one case—the piano voices of the third canon—invert and retrograde-invert it. The voices are paired (three pairs in the final canon, two in the others), the subsequent pair(s) having the same rhythmic structure as the first but accelerated so that they end together. (Such so-called "mensuration" canons are common in fifteenth-century music, a point Davies underscores in choosing quotations.)

The three canons are separated by brief melodic fragments in the cello, the first of which (mm. 19–21) quotes a fragment from Davies's own *Ecce manus tradentis,* a composition for solo voices, chorus, and instruments written a few years earlier. (The quote was anticipated in the viola in m. 7, the opening seventh imitating the two cello sevenths at the beginning of the measure.) The fragment, derived from the whole-tone tetrachord B-C♯-D♯-E♯, associates closely with the canonic voices. The movement ends, as do the others, with ritualistic bells.

Davies has said of No. 6, "The Mocking of Christ," that "the 'mocking' is effected inside the music entirely." The movement opens with a brief aleatory segment in which four instruments enter one by one, playing small groups of notes freely and in varying order (the pitches are taken from the fourth movement). This serves as an introduction, overlapping briefly with, in Davies's words, "a garbled Victorian hymn (a musical style which I consider almost the ultimate blasphemy)," performed by the dancer on an out-of-tune "barroom" piano in a clumsy, heavily doubled harmonization (m. 236*a*). Here the parodistic aspect reaches new levels. The hymn quotes a passage from Davies's own *Missa super L'homme armé* for voice and chamber ensemble, composed the previous year; that work is based on an anonymous fifteenth-century mass, and the mass is in turn based on the popular medieval song *L'homme armé.* To top things off, the Victorian hymn is a Davies harmonization of a melodic line taken from the anonymous mass.

At m. 235*b* the introductory music returns, joined by a xylophone, leading to a variation on the hymn, reincarnated as a fox-trot (m. 236*b*). The movement ends with a new set of repeating instrumental figures that overlap with the fox-trot, then degenerate into a single repeated measure played by the ensemble pianist, merging into a final, repeated dissonant chord. Transitional arpeggiations lead to the next movement.

No. 8, "St. Veronica Wipes His Face," is a musical representation of the story of St. Veronica, who, having wiped Christ's brow with her kerchief, finds the image of his face permanently imprinted on it. The movement contains various types of "reproduced" musical images, taking its departure from the cello quotation from *Ecce manus tradentis* first heard in No. 1, which is subjected to a series of distortions and transformations, never appearing exactly as it was. The cello quotation is first heard lyrically, with an elaborate arpeggiated accompaniment, which Davies likens to a "Victorian daguerreotype" (an early type of photograph). At m. 262 it appears briefly in its original form (flute), then wildly distorted (viola). In m. 263 it occurs in conjunction with sustained lines in the flute and clarinet, likened by the composer to a Schenkerian analysis in reverse, taking on more and more detail until eventually it suggests a passage from the Scherzo of Beethoven's Fifth Symphony (mm. 273–76). At m. 278 the quotation is again transformed, here into the opening of the Scherzo from Beethoven's Ninth ("a related but false image," Davies notes).

This phantasmagorical succession finally introduces (m. 280) a more extensive quotation, from Pierre de la Rue's *Missa L'homme armé*[2]—*not,* then, the anonymous mass based on the same popular song evoked in the first movement, but another one, which also recalls the first movement in its use of mensuration canon. (The *L'homme armé* song first appears in the tenor of the piano part, then is transferred to the viola at m. 283.) The entire first section of the La Rue appears complete, but distorted through instrumental exchanges, doublings, and rhythmic and registral displacements, plus a typewriter's percussive comment. A final "photographic reproduction" overlaps with its concluding D-minor cadence (m. 294): the return of the opening *Ecce manus tradentis* fragment (mm. 259–62), which, having been recorded during the performance on a "cheap commercial tape recorder," is played back. This gives way to a music box, its motives quietly imitated by the musicians, and a concluding chord.

The extravagant finale, "Resurrection—Antichrist," is described by Davies as "going all Hollywood and ridiculous." Here the original story is altered: it is not Christ who emerges from the tomb but the Antichrist, "the dark 'double' of Christ of medieval legend, indistinguishable from the 'real' Christ." This, then, is the ultimate twist of identity. "Some may consider [it] sacrilegious," Davies has remarked, "but the point I am trying to make is a moral one: it is a matter of distinguishing the false from the real, that one should not be taken in by appearances." The music of the finale is based on the fox-trot version of the Victorian hymn from No. 6, to which a rakish swing melody is added, played by the viola in parallel sixths and thirds, supported by the clarinet and flute. The entire hymn progression returns, elaborated, and is repeated, closing with a much-reiterated cadential figure that finally ends with a C-major chord with added lower seventh (the ultimate cliché). The close brings a last reference to Davies's "own" music: a pure whole-tone chord in the piano, followed by a whole-tone cello fragment, played pizzicato.

2.   The segment quoted is the opening of the Kyrie I, which may be found in Archibald T. Davison and Willi Apel, eds., *Historical Anthology of Music* (Cambridge, 1954), p. 95.

29

STEVE REICH (b. 1936)
Music for Pieces of Wood (1973)

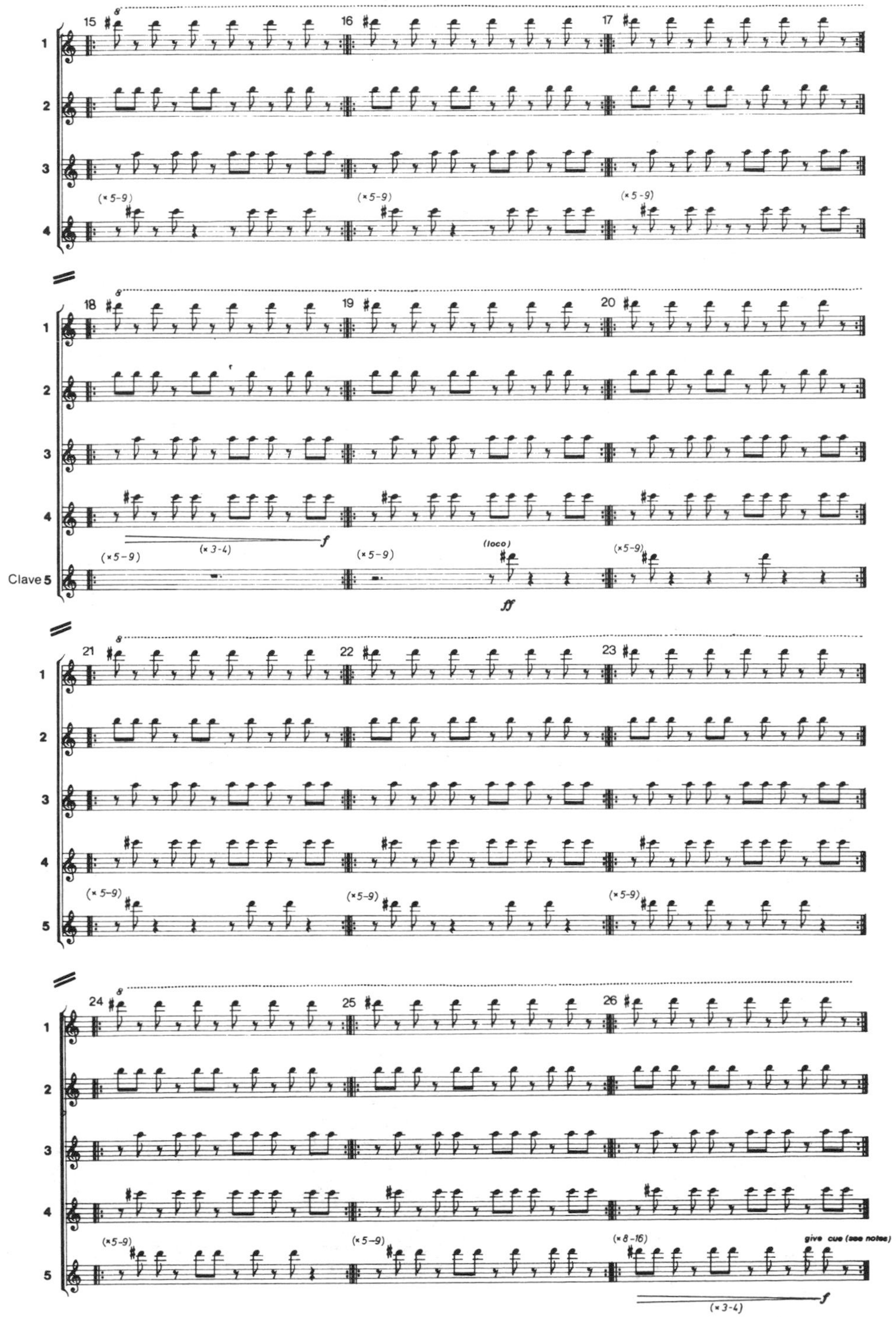
Clave 5
(×5-9)
(×3-4)
(loco)
ff
f
(×8-16)
give cue (see notes)

Notes on Performance

Repeats

The number of repeats of each bar is not fixed. It may vary within the approximate limits marked in each bar, e.g. bar 1 may be repeated 2–4 times, then claves two enter at bar 2 for about 4–6 repeats and so on. The *indications* for approximate numbers of repeats are written above the part which is responsible for making the particular change in each bar, e.g. player 3 is responsible for bars 3 through 10 (since players one and two repeat without changing during those bars) and consequently the approximate number of repeats (5–9) is written above player three's part, and similarly throughout the piece.

At bar 10 there are two repeat markings, for player three to fade gradually from *ff* to *f* in about 3–4 repeats and for player four to rest 5–9 repeats before entering at bar 11. Similar instances occur at bar 18 and 26 and later in the piece. At bar 27 players three, four and five all fade out together taking about 4–6 repeats to do so. They should simply rehearse this and listen to one another so that they can fade out together, and similarly at bar 45.

The point throughout is not to focus on counting repeats but to listen to each bar and when you hear that a particular pattern has become clear and absorbed by yourself and the audience, move on to the next bar.

Cues

At bar 26 player five, after 8–16 repeats nods his or her head on the downbeat as a cue for players three and four to repeat bar 26 two more times and then move into bar 27. A similar cue is given by player five at bar 44, and at the last bar after 24–48 repeats player five nods on the downbeat, all players repeat the bar twice and end together. If desired another player can give the cues.

Claves and Tuning

The claves required for the steady pulse in part one are the usual cylindrical solid claves and should be readily available. This clave is held in the conventional way, resting on a partially closed hand so that it can resonate.

The clave used as a beater need not be tuned, but the one struck should be tuned to the high D♯ written in the score in part one. Since it will be easiest to tune this kind of clave by sanding its end with a power sander to make it *shorter and thus higher in pitch* one should either find a clave tuned exactly to the high D♯, or one tuned below that and tune it sharp by sanding it shorter.

The claves required for parts 2 through 5 are at least an octave lower in pitch and are of two special types manufactured by: The Latin Percussion Co. Inc., P.O. Box 88, Palisades Park, New Jersey 07650, U.S.A. Claves 2 and 3 are that company's 'African' model LP 212 A, and claves 4 and 5 are their 'Standard' model LP 211. These claves will also have to be tuned by power sanding them *shorter* to make them *sharper*, and by sanding the bevel in the center of these claves somewhat *deeper* to make them *flatter* in pitch. It should be noted that considerable sanding of the ends must be done to make the claves noticeably rise in pitch whereas just a slight sanding and deepening of the bevel will produce considerable lowering of the pitch.

The tuning of the entire set of claves should preferably be to the exact pitches written in the score, however it is possible to transpose them up or down a bit so long as the relative pitch relationships remain the same.

The 'African' and 'Standard' claves should be held rather tightly with the hand cupped under the bevel to produce a resonating chamber. Without a solid grip a poor sound will result with little pitch content, and performers should practise perfecting their grip so as to form a resonating chamber tightly closed at the front of the bevel and open at its rear to produce a deep rich timbre with a clear pitch. Both types of claves are pictured below.

'African' clave   'Standard' clave

Using substitute instruments is generally discouraged. Various substitutes have been tried but all seem clearly inferior to the claves described above. Specifically, crotales or brass antique cymbals have been tried using a single crotale firmly held by leather or nylon cord through its hole in one hand and struck with a hard rubber or wooden mallet with the other hand while sitting, and damped on the thigh on all rests. The timbre of these crotales (though their pitch is clear) can quickly become excessively shrill. Tuned cow bells are lower in pitch and not shrill. They should also be played while sitting so as to allow damping on the thigh on all rests. This damping, while necessary to create clear articulation, will necessitate a slower tempo. The xylophone could conceivably be used with perhaps only 3 performers, two with 2 mallets and one with 1, but the xylophone produces too 'thin' a sound lacking the 'weight' of the claves. Temple blocks could be possibly used for the lower 4 parts, but would have to be tuned which may prove difficult.

Performers are urged to find and tune the claves mentioned above if at all possible.

Performers may stand while playing as illustrated in the drawing and photo below which will allow them to hear and see each other clearly.

Duration

The duration of the piece may vary from about 11 to 15 minutes.

ANALYTICAL COMMENTS

Steve Reich's "phase" compositions of the late 1960s and early 1970s played a significant role in the development of musical minimalism. The earliest such works involved very gradual phase shifts: one of two or more identical patterns played in unison would slightly accelerate so as to move gradually out of phase with the others. After 1971, however, Reich began to favor abrupt phase shifts rather than gradual ones, and instead of beginning with complete patterns, he built up patterns one note at a time. "Gradualism" was thus preserved, but relocated from the process of phase shifting to the process of pattern accumulation.

Music for Pieces of Wood represents this second stage of phase composition. It is also, like all Reich's phase pieces, an instance of "process" composition; that is, it is based on a constructive mechanism that, once set in motion, generates essentially automatically both the note-by-note succession and the overall form. To some extent this process resembles serialism, though the systematic aspects are here much less complex, and are linked to relatively simple, constantly repeated patterns, making them much easier to follow aurally.

The piece is composed for five pairs of tuned claves, instruments that are very similar in timbre and thus assure a unified overall effect, yet distinguishable by relative highness or lowness. In his "Notes on Performance" (on a separate page here following the score), Reich describes the optimum instruments (raising the possibility, though discouraging it, of substituting other instruments), and discusses measure repetitions, which are variable within prescribed limits. The allowance for choice in the repetition of measures has less to do with musical "indeterminacy," however, than with creating a performance context that encourages ensemble cooperation.

Music for Pieces of Wood contains three segments of diminishing length: mm. 1–28, 29–46, and 47–59. The first clave performs uninterrupted *forte* attacks throughout, linking all three sections with its undifferentiated quarter-note metrical pattern, against which the "motivic" patterns are juxtaposed. (The first clave's separation from the rest of the ensemble is emphasized by its considerably higher pitch.) The basic rhythmic pattern, which provides all the material used in the composition, is introduced in m. 2. It contains eight eighth-note attacks distributed within twelve eighth notes (the notated 6/4 meter), the number of successive attacks separated by rests forming a symmetrical pattern: $3+2+1+2+3$ (the last 3 occur when the pattern is repeated). The second clave plays this pattern *forte* throughout the first section.

A cumulative phase-shifting process begins in m. 3 with the third clave's *fortissimo* attack on a single eighth. Over the next seven measures an additional attack appears in each measure, ending with the completion of the pattern of eight attacks at m. 10, joined with a diminuendo to *forte* (bringing the third clave to the dynamic level of the second). The pattern generated by the third clave is not in phase with that of the second, however, but starts with the seventh eighth note of the original pattern (a rest) rather than the first (Example 1).

EXAMPLE 1

At m. 11 the fourth clave initiates a similar process, entering *fortissimo* with a single attack and gradually adding one per measure until it completes the pattern at m. 18, again with a diminuendo to *forte*. The fourth clave's pattern is in phase with the third's, although it is built up through a different sequence of attacks. The fifth clave, the last to play, begins the same process in m. 19, completing its pattern—in phase with the first clave—at m. 26. As the first segment's overall process is completed, the four main instruments are thus playing only two different phases. All return to the original phase in the following measure (m. 27), ending the segment as claves three through five fade into silence.

M. 28 is transitional. The second clave retains the original pattern (and thus omits the diminuendo in m. 27), bringing things back to where they were in m. 2 and providing a point of reference for the derivation of the second segment's pattern. This second segment, appearing in m. 29, is formed by dropping the three successive eighth notes plus the following rest (i.e., the first four eighths) from the original, which reduces the content to five attacks distributed in eight eighth notes (the notated 4/4 measure). The same developmental process then unfolds as before. Since there are only five attacks in the pattern, the accumulations in claves three through five require only five measures, accelerating the unfolding structure (countered, however, by an increase in the number of repetitions allowed per measure). Another difference is that the fourth clave no longer duplicates the third's phase but has its own, so that there are three simultaneous phases rather than two at the end of this segment (m. 44).

As at the close of the first segment, the next measure (m. 45) contains a unison restatement of the original phase of the pattern, with a fade to silence in claves three through five, followed by an isolated restatement in clave one (m. 46). The latter is again followed by a new pattern (m. 47) derived from the previous one through compression—the single eighth attack plus the following rest (the fourth and fifth eighth) are omitted, which reduces the figure to four attacks distributed in six eighths (the notated 3/4 measure).

The developmental process begins a final time at m. 48, once more structurally accelerated (now requiring only four measures to complete the patterns in claves three through five, though again countered by an increase in repetitions per measure). As in the preceding section, the fourth clave has its own phase, so that there are three different phases at the end. Despite the absence of a unison restatement of the original phase (as at mm. 27 and 45), a "cadential" character is achieved by allowing the final measure to be repeated more times than any other measure in the composition (up to forty-eight).

The extremely repetitious quality of the piece, along with the very gradual surface transformations produced by additions of a single note per measure, typify Reich's music. *Music for Pieces of Wood* nevertheless has a definite developmental and goal-directed shape, both within segments (where notes gradually accumulate to a point of maximum density) and overall (where the contractions of the basic pattern and the phase accumulations create a strong sense of forward direction). Somewhat at odds with the static, non-developmental character of the composer's previous work, the composition provides early evidence of the more traditional course Reich's music would follow in subsequent years.

Appendix A

READING AN ORCHESTRAL SCORE

CLEFS

The music for some instruments is written in clefs other than the familiar treble and bass. In the following example, middle C is shown in the four clefs used in orchestral scores:

Treble   Alto   Tenor   Bass
clef   clef   clef   clef

The *alto clef* is primarily used in viola parts. The *tenor clef* is employed for cello, bassoon, and trombone parts when these instruments play in a high register.

TRANSPOSING INSTRUMENTS

The music for some instruments is customarily written at a pitch different from their actual sound. The following list, with examples, shows the main transposing instruments and the degree of transposition.

Instrument	Transposition	Written Note	Actual Sound
Piccolo / Celesta	sound an octave higher than written		
Trumpet in F	sound a fourth higher than written		
Trumpet in E	sound a major third higher than written		
Clarinet in E♭ / Trumpet in E♭	sound a minor third higher than written		
Trumpet in D / Clarinet in D	sound a major second higher than written		

Clarinet in B♭
Trumpet in B♭
Cornet in B♭
Horn in B♭ alto

sound a major second
lower than written

Clarinet in A
Trumpet in A
Cornet in A

sound a minor third
lower than written

Horn in G
Alto flute

sound a fourth
lower than written

English horn
Horn in F

sound a fifth
lower than written

Horn in E

sound a minor sixth
lower than written

Horn in E♭

sound a major sixth
lower than written

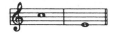

Horn in D

sound a minor seventh
lower than written

Contrabassoon
Horn in C
Double bass

sound an octave
lower than written

Bass clarinet in B♭
(written in treble clef)

sound a major ninth
lower than written

(written in bass clef)

sound a major second
lower than written

Bass clarinet in A
(written in treble clef)

sound a minor tenth
lower than written

(written in bass clef)

sound a minor third
lower than written

Appendix B

INSTRUMENTAL NAMES AND ABBREVIATIONS

The following tables set forth the English, Italian, German, and French names used for the various musical instruments in these scores, and their respective abbreviations. A table of the foreign-language names for scale degrees and modes is also provided.

WOODWINDS

English	Italian	German	French
Piccolo (Picc.)	Flauto piccolo (Fl. Picc.)	Kleine Flöte (Kl. Fl.)	Petite flûte
Flute (Fl.)	Flauto (Fl.); Flauto grande (Fl. gr.)	Grosse Flöte (Fl. gr.)	Flûte (Fl.)
Alto flute	Flauto contralto (fl.c-alto)	Altflöte	Flûte en sol
Oboe (Ob.)	Oboe (Ob.)	Hoboe (Hb.); Oboe (Ob.)	Hautbois (Hb.)
English horn (E. H.)	Corno inglese (C. or Cor. ingl., C.i.)	Englisches Horn (E. H.)	Cor anglais (C. a.)
Sopranino clarinet	Clarinetto piccolo (clar. picc.)		
Clarinet (C., Cl., Clt., Clar.)	Clarinetto (Cl. Clar.)	Klarinette (Kl.)	Clarinette (Cl.)
Bass clarinet (B. Cl.)	Clarinetto basso (Cl. b., Cl. basso, Clar. basso)	Bass Klarinette (Bkl.)	Clarinette basse (Cl. bs.)
Bassoon (Bsn., Bssn.)	Fagotto (Fag., Fg.)	Fagott (Fag., Fg.)	Basson (Bssn.)
Contrabassoon (C. Bsn.)	Contrafagotto (Cfg., C. Fag., Cont. F.)	Kontrafagott (Kfg.)	Contrebasson (C. bssn.)

BRASS

English	Italian	German	French
French horn (Hr., Hn.)	Corno (Cor., C.)	Horn (Hr.) [*pl.* Hörner (Hrn.)]	Cor; Cor à pistons
Trumpet (Tpt., Trpt., Trp., Tr.)	Tromba (Tr.)	Trompete (Tr., Trp.)	Trompette (Tr.)
Trumpet in D	Tromba piccola (Tr. picc.)		
Cornet	Cornetta	Kornett	Cornet à pistons (C. à p., Pist.)
Trombone (Tr., Tbe., Trb., Trm., Trbe.)	Trombone [*pl.* Tromboni (Tbni., Trni.)]	Posaune (Ps., Pos.)	Trombone (Tr.)
Tuba (Tb.)	Tuba (Tb, Tba.)	Tuba (Tb.) [*also* Basstuba (Btb.)]	Tuba (Tb.)

PERCUSSION

English	Italian	German	French
Percussion (Perc.)	Percussione	Schlagzeug (Schlag.)	Batterie (Batt.)
Kettledrums (K. D.)	Timpani (Timp., Tp.)	Pauken (Pk.)	Timbales (Timb.)
Snare drum (S. D.)	Tamburo piccolo (Tamb. picc.) . Tamburo militare (Tamb. milit.)	Kleine Trommel (Kl. Tr.)	Caisse claire (C. cl.), Caisse roulante Tambour militaire (Tamb. milit.)
Bass drum (B. drum)	Gran cassa (Gr. Cassa, Gr. C., G. C.)	Grosse Trommel (Gr. Tr.)	Grosse caisse (Gr. c.)
Cymbals (Cym., Cymb.)	Piatti (P., Ptti., Piat.)	Becken (Beck.)	Cymbales (Cym.)
Tam-Tam (Tam-T.)			
Tambourine (Tamb.)	Tamburino (Tamb.)	Schellentrommel, Tamburin	Tambour de Basque (T. de B., Tamb. de Basque)
Triangle (Trgl., Tri.)	Triangolo (Trgl.)	Triangel	Triangle (Triang.)
Glockenspiel (Glocken.)	Campanelli (Cmp.)	Glockenspiel	Carillon
Bells (Chimes)	Campane (Cmp.)	Glocken	Cloches

Antique Cymbals	Crotali Piatti antichi	Antiken Zimbeln	Cymbales antiques
Sleigh Bells	Sonagli (Son.)	Schellen	Grelots
Xylophone (Xyl.)	Xilofono	Xylophon	Xylophone
Cowbells		Herdenglocken	

Crash cymbal	Grande cymbale chinoise
Siren	Sirène
Lion's roar	Tambour à corde
Slapstick	Fouet
Wood blocks	Blocs chinois

STRINGS

English	Italian	German	French
Violin (V., Vl., Vln, Vi.)	Violino (V., Vl., Vln.)	Violine (V., Vl., Vln.) Geige (Gg.)	Violon (V., Vl., Vln.)
Viola (Va., Vl., *pl.* Vas.)	Viola (Va., Vla.) *pl.* Viole (Vle.)	Bratsche (Br.)	Alto (A.)
Violoncello, Cello (Vcl., Vc.)	Violoncello (Vc., Vlc., Vcllo.)	Violoncell (Vc., (Vlc.)	Violoncelle (Vc.)
Double bass (D. Bs.)	Contrabasso (Cb., C. B.) *pl.* Contrabassi or Bassi (C. Bassi, Bi.)	Kontrabass (Kb.)	Contrebasse (C. B.)

OTHER INSTRUMENTS

English	Italian	German	French
Harp (Hp., Hrp.)	Arpa (A., Arp.)	Harfe (Hrf.)	Harpe (Hp.)
Piano	Pianoforte (P.-f., Pft.)	Klavier	Piano
Celesta (Cel.)			
Harpsichord	Cembalo	Cembalo	Clavecin
Harmonium (Harmon.)			
Organ (Org.)	Organo	Orgel	Orgue
Guitar		Gitarre (Git.)	
Mandoline (Mand.)			

NAMES OF SCALE DEGREES AND MODES

SCALE DEGREES

English	Italian	German	French
C	do	C	ut
C-sharp	do diesis	Cis	ut dièse
D-flat	re bemolle	Des	ré bémol
D	re	D	ré
D-sharp	re diesis	Dis	ré dièse
E-flat	mi bemolle	Es	mi bémol
E	mi	E	mi
E-sharp	mi diesis	Eis	mi dièse
F-flat	fa bemolle	Fes	fa bémol
F	fa	F	fa
F-sharp	fa diesis	Fis	fa dièse
G-flat	sol bemolle	Ges	sol bémol
G	sol	G	sol
G-sharp	sol diesis	Gis	sol dièse
A-flat	la bemolle	As	la bémol
A	la	A	la
A-sharp	la diesis	Ais	la dièse
B-flat	si bemolle	B	si bémol
B	si	H	si
B-sharp	si diesis	His	si dièse
C-flat	do bemolle	Ces	ut bémol

MODES

major	maggiore	dur	majeur
minor	minore	moll	mineur

Appendix C

GLOSSARY OF TERMS IN THE SCORES

This glossary includes only terms found in this anthology. One common form of a word is given ("dolce"); the reader can easily deduce the meaning of its variations ("dolcissimo"). Omitted are foreign terms very similar to English ones ("intenso") or in common use ("solo"). Extended and highly individualized instructions from the composer to the performer are translated on the music itself. Please refer to Appendix B for names of musical instruments.

a. To, at, with
ab. Off
abwechselndes, chorisches Atmen. Alternating, choral breathing
accelerando. Becoming faster
adagio. Slow, leisurely
ad libitum (ad lib). At the discretion of the performer
agitato. Agitated, excited
allargando. Becoming broader
allegretto. A moderately fast tempo
allegro. A rapid tempo (between allegretto and presto)
am Frosch. At the frog
am Griffbrett. On the fingerboard
am Steg. On the bridge
andante. A moderately slow tempo (between adagio and allegretto)
an der Spitze. At the point
animato, animando. Animated
à partir du 4me temps. From the fourth beat
arco. Played with the bow
assai. Very
ausklingen lassen. Let vibrate
äusserst. Extremely
avec la main. With the hand

battute (batt.). Beat, rhythm
begleitend. Accompanying
ben. Very
betont. Accented
bewegt. Agitated
bocca chiusa. Mouth closed
breiter. Broader
breve. Short

cantabile. In a singing style
chiaro. Clear, evident
col legno. With the wood
come sopra. As before
comme un cri. Like a cry
con. With
con slancio. Dashingly
corda. String
court. Short
crescendo (cresc.). Becoming louder
cuivré. Brassy

Dämpfer. Mute
dans un sentiment sourd et tumultueux. Heavily and tumultuously

445

deciso. Decisive
deutlich. Clear, distinct
diminuendo (dim.). Becoming softer
divisi (div.). Divided
dolce. Sweet, gentle
dolente. Doleful
doppio. Double
durch Flag. erzeugen. Produce with harmonics

en dehors. Bring out
espressivo, expressivo. Expressive.
etwas. Somewhat
étouffée. Stopped

flautando. Flute-like
fliessend. Flowing
flüchtig. Flighty
Flatterzunge (flttzg). Fluttertongue
fortsetzend. Continuing
frapper. Strike
frottées l'une contre l'autre. Rubbed one against the other
frotter rudement la membrane avec la pouce. Rub the skin roughly with the thumb
fuoco. Force

gemächlich. Soft, slow, comfortable
geschlagen. Struck
geschwind. Quick
gestopt. Stopped
gestrichen. Bowed
gewöhnlich. Usual
giovale. Jovial
glissando. Gliding quickly over successive notes
grave. Heavy, strong
grazioso. Graceful

haletantes. Panting
heftiger. Heavier
hervortreten. Bring out
hurlant. Howling

immer. Always

klingt. Sounds
kurz. Short

laissez. Let
langsam. Slow
largamente. Broadly
largo. A very slow tempo
lebhaft. Lively
legato (leg.). Smooth
legèrement, leggiero, leicht. Lightly
lento. A slow tempo (between andante and largo)
loco. Return
longue, lunga. Long, sustained
lourd. Heavy
l.v. Let vibrate

ma. But
maestoso. Majestic
marcato. With emphasis
mässig. Moderate
m.d. Right hand
meno. Less
mesto. Sad
m.g. or *m.s.* Left hand
mit. With
mit dünnen Metallstab. With thin metal rod
mit Ton. With style
moderato. At a moderate tempo
modo. Manner
molto. Very much
morendo. Dying away
mosso. Rapid

niente. Nothing
noch. Still
notiert. Notated

offen, ouvert. Open
ogni suono. Each sound
ohne. Without
ordinario (ord.). In the ordinary way (cancelling a special instruction)

parte. Part
pedalton. Pedal note
per. By, through
pesante. Heavily
piqué. Staccato
più. More
pizzicato (pizz.). Plucked
plötzlich. Suddenly
poco. Little
portamento. A continuous movement from one pitch to another

précédente. Previous
précisément. Exactly
presto. A very quick tempo (faster than allegro)

quasi. Almost

rallentando. Becoming slower
rasch. Quick
rebord. Rim
recitando. Recited
recitative. A singing style imitating speech
ritardando. Slowing
ritenuto. Holding back in speed
ruhiger. Calmer

Saite. String
Schallrichter hoch. Bells up
scherzando, scherzoso. Playfully
schliesslich. Finally
schnell. Fast
sec, secco. Dry
secouer. To shake
serré. Pressed
sehr. Very
s'éteindre. Extinguish
semplice. In a simple manner
sempre. Always
senza. Without
sforzando (sfz, sf). With sudden emphasis
simile. In a similar manner
sonore. Sound
sordino. Mute
sostenuto. Sustained
sotto voce. In an undertone
sourdement. Muted
spring. Bog. Bounced bow
staccato. Detached
steigernd. Intensifying
stesso. Same

stets weich, ohne Akzent einsetzen. Always soft, entering without accent
strepitoso. Noisy
stretto. Increasing speed (of a concluding section of a non-fugal work)
stringendo. Quickening
subito. Suddenly
sul ponticello. On the bridge

tacet. Be silent
tenuto. Held, sustained
tornare. Return
tremolo. Rapid reiteration of one or more notes
très. Very
troppo. Too much
tutti. All

unis., unisono. Unison

verlöschend. Dying out
vibrer. Vibrate
viel. Much
vivace, vivo. Lively
voilé. Subdued
voll. Full
vuota. Open, empty

weicher Filzschlegel. Soft, felt stick
wenig. Little
wieder. Again

zart. Gently
Zeitmass. Tempo
ziemlich. Somewhat
zu. Too
zurückhaltend. Slackening in speed.
zurückkehren. Return

Index A

FORMS AND GENRES

Index B

ANALYTIC CATEGORIES